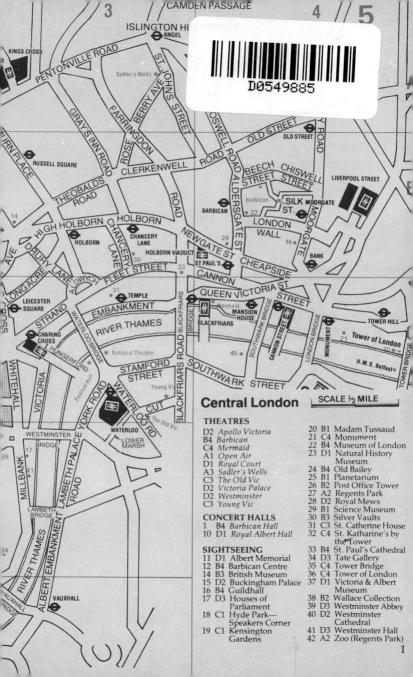

Central London

SCALE ½ MILE

THEATRES

- D2 Apollo Victoria
- B4 Barbican
- C4 Mermaid
- A1 Open Air
- D1 Royal Court
- A3 Sadler's Wells
- C3 The Old Vic
- D2 Victoria Palace
- D2 Westminster
- C3 Young Vic

CONCERT HALLS

- 1 B4 Barbican Hall
- 10 D1 Royal Albert Hall

SIGHTSEEING

- 11 D1 Albert Memorial
- 12 B4 Barbican Centre
- 14 B3 British Museum
- 15 D2 Buckingham Palace
- 16 B4 Guildhall
- 17 D3 Houses of Parliament
- 18 C1 Hyde Park—Speakers Corner
- 19 C1 Kensington Gardens
- 20 B1 Madam Tussaud
- 21 C4 Monument
- 22 B4 Museum of London
- 23 D1 Natural History Museum
- 24 B4 Old Bailey
- 25 B1 Planetarium
- 26 B2 Post Office Tower
- 27 A2 Regents Park
- 28 D2 Royal Mews
- 29 B1 Science Museum
- 30 B3 Silver Vaults
- 31 C3 St. Catherine House
- 32 C4 St. Katharine's by the Tower
- 33 B4 St. Paul's Cathedral
- 34 D3 Tate Gallery
- 35 C4 Tower Bridge
- 36 C4 Tower of London
- 37 D1 Victoria & Albert Museum
- 38 B2 Wallace Collection
- 39 D3 Westminster Abbey
- 40 D2 Westminster Cathedral
- 41 D3 Westminster Hall
- 42 A2 Zoo (Regents Park)

1

Setting the Scene

Whether your trip to London is giving you the opportunity to revive treasured memories or embark upon an exciting 'voyage of discovery', it's almost certain that somewhere in your itinerary will be featured an outing to the theatre or concert hall. For nowhere else in the world is concentrated such a wide variety of entertainment in such a charming and historical 'theatrical capital'!

It was to help visitors and residents alike to find their way through the maze of London's theatreland that 'The London Theatre Scene' was born. Now into its third edition, it has been completely revised and updated offering even more comprehensive information for theatregoers — booking details, seating plans, suggestions for convenient places to meet, eat and drink —plus nearby hotels. (Easy to read street maps for every section!)

THE LONDON THEATRE SCENE

Susie Elms

FRANK COOK PUBLICATIONS

Whilst every care has been taken to ensure accuracy the publisher cannot be held responsible for errors resulting from inaccurate information received.

Published and produced by Frank Cook Travel Guides,
8 Wykeham Court, Old Perry Street, Chislehurst, Kent BR7 6PN
Written by Susan Elms — Illustrated by Clive Desmond
Printed in Britain by CW Printing, Kent.
Phototypeset by Keyset Video Ltd., Woolwich SE18.

London maps by Peter Hale, based on the Ordnance Survey Map with the sanction of the Controller of Her Majesty's Stationery Office, copyright reserved.

Copyright © 1979 Frank Cook Travel Guides. All rights reserved. (3rd Edition 1985)

In compiling this Guide we would like to make particular mention of the following publications which have proved invaluable to our research:

"The Theatres of London" by Raymond Mander and Joe Mitchenson,
"Victorian & Edwardian Theatres" by Victor Glasstone,
"The Penguin Dictionary of Theatre" by John Russell Taylor.
Lytton's Theatre Seating Plans published by the Dancing Times Lda.

We would also like to thank The Society of West End Theatre for their interest and valuable assistance.

ISBN 0 9506503 2 3

Contents

Theatres and Concert Halls

The Society of West End Theatre

London Fringe Theatres

Where to Eat

Where to Stay

Transport

THE SOCIETY OF WEST END THEATRE AT YOUR SERVICE.

THE LONDON THEATRE GUIDE

Published every two weeks, the London Theatre Guide is the definitive and comprehensive listing of West End Theatre productions, encompassing all the information needed to make that visit to the theatre complete. It contains details of the many productions available to the theatregoer including performance length and times, information on those theatres operating the Student Standby and Senior Citizens Matinee schemes plus an indication of the facilities available for the disabled in each theatre. The Guide may be obtained free of charge at West End theatres, Tourist Information Centres, Public Libraries etc, it is also available on subscription.

WEST END THEATRE MAGAZINE

The first official journal of The Society of West End Theatre, this magazine offers the reader lively and interesting articles on all aspects of the theatre and theatregoing, star interviews, hints on fashion, restaurant and book reviews, details of both current and forthcoming productions — even an outline of the plot! information on ticket prices and transport.

An annual subscription to this bi-monthly publication will also secure a host of special discounts and offers available exclusively to the subscriber.

HOW TO BOOK YOUR THEATRE SEATS

This informative leaflet identifies the various ways of booking tickets for West End theatre productions.

WHERE TO EAT

Not only does this leaflet offer a selection of the many restaurants in theatreland, it also gives an idea of the prices one might expect to pay, plus a map showing the relationship of the restaurants to the theatres.

TRAINS AND THE THEATREGOER

A new leaflet giving details and times of the last trains from London stations proving without doubt that it is possible to visit the theatre, have time for a meal or drink after the performance and still be able to catch a train home.

SENIOR CITIZENS MATINEE SCHEME

A leaflet explaining this popular scheme which makes certain matinee performances available to Senior Citizens at reduced prices.

OTHER LEAFLETS

THE LAURENCE OLIVIER AWARDS — see page 64
WEST END THEATRE TOKENS — see page 99
LEICESTER SQUARE HALF-PRICE TICKET BOOTH —
see page 98

For further information and copies of any of the above leaflets, please write (enclosing a stamped addressed envelope) to:

The Society of West End Theatre,
Bedford Chambers, Covent Garden Piazza, London WC2E 8HQ.

THE LONDON THEATRE. ACT ON IT

Theatres — Concert Halls

Index and Box Office Telephone Numbers:-
(please add prefix 01 when dialling from outside the London area)

Theatres

Concert Halls

Outer London theatres

Ashcroft, Park Lane, Croydon, Surrey.   Tel: 688 9291.
Churchill, High Street, Bromley, Kent.   Tel: 460 6677.
Greenwich, Crooms Hill, SE10.   Tel: 858 7755.   —4447 —3800
Hampstead, Swiss Cottage Centre, NW3.   Tel: 722 9301.
Richmond, The Green, Richmond, Surrey.   Tel: 940 0088.
Round House, Chalk Farm Road, NW1.   Tel: 267 2564.
Shaw, 100 Euston Road, NW1.   Tel: 388 1394.
Wimbledon, The Broadway, Wimbledon, SW19.   Tel: 542 2883.

⤷ Box Office: 540 - 0363

13 Nevada St.

Maps

Every entry in this guide is pinpointed on detailed street maps pages:
1, 10-17 and pages 149-161.

Symbols:

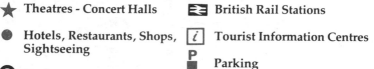

★ Theatres - Concert Halls

● Hotels, Restaurants, Shops, Sightseeing

⊖ Underground Stations

⊞ British Rail Stations

[i] Tourist Information Centres

P▪ Parking

Central London

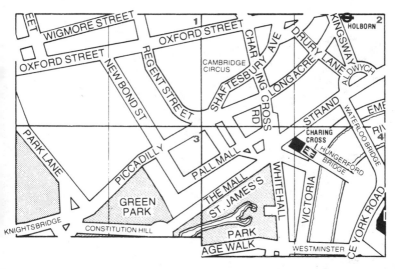

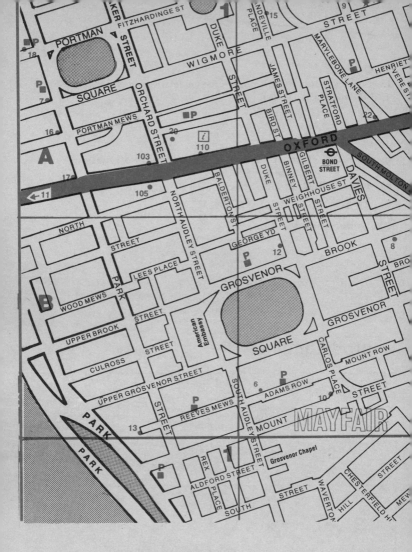

HOTELS:

5	A4	Berners	12	B2	Europa	18	A1	Portman
6	B2	Britannia	13	B1	Grosvenor	19	B4	Regent Palace
7	A1	Churchill	14	A2	Londoner	20	A1	Selfridge
8	B2	Claridges	15	A2	Mandeville	21	A3	St. George's
9	A2	Clifton Ford	16	A1	Mostyn	22	A2	Stratford Court
10	B2	Connaught	17	A1	Mount Royal	23	B3	Westbury
11	A1	Cumberland						

THEATRES:

1 A4 *London Palladium*
2 B4 *Piccadilly*
4 A2 *Wigmore Hall*

SHOPPING:

71   B4 Aquascutum
85   A4 Dickens & Jones
86   A3 D. H. Evans
91   A4 Hamley Bros.
96   A4 Jaeger
99   A3 John Lewis
101 A4 Liberty
103 A1 Marks & Spencer
105 A1 Mothercare
110 A1 Selfridges

SIGHTSEEING:

119 A4 Carnaby Street
120 B4 Museum of Mankind

13

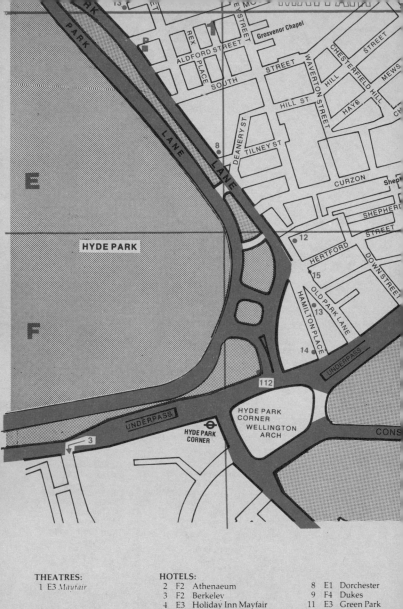

THEATRES:
1 E3 *Mayfair*

HOTELS:

2	F2	Athenaeum
3	F2	Berkeley
4	E3	Holiday Inn Mayfair
5	E3	Brown's
6	E4	Cavendish
7	E2	Chesterfield

8	E1	Dorchester
9	F4	Dukes
11	E3	Green Park
12	F2	Hilton
13	F2	Inn On The Park
14	F2	Intercontinental

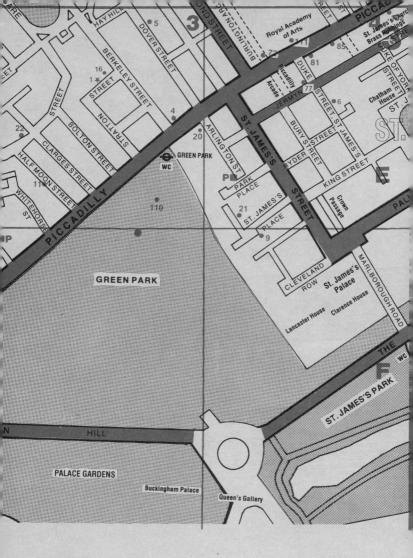

THEATRES:

1 G5 *Haymarket, Theatre Royal*
2 G5 *Her Majesty's*
3 G8 *National*
      Olivier
      Lyttelton
      Cottesloe
4 G8 *Festival Hall*
5 G8 *Purcell*
6 G8 *Queen Elizabeth*
7 G8 *National Film*
8 G6 *Whitehall*

HOTELS:

10 G6 Charing Cross
11 G6 Royal Adelphi
12 G7 Royal Horseguard
13 G5 Royal Trafalgar

RESTAURANTS:
:0	G5	A L'ecu de France
:3	G5, G7	McDonald's
:4	G5	Rowleys
83	G6	Sherlock Holmes

SHOPPING:
41	G5	Burberry's
43	G5	Design Centre

SIGHTSEEING:
51	G8	Hayward Gallery
52	G6	National Gallery
53	G6	National Portrait Gallery

How to book seats for London's Theatres

Booking in advance will guarantee obtaining seats for the show and performance of your choice at the price you want to pay, thus avoiding disappointment.

Five ways to book your seat

● Go directly to the Theatre Box Office — generally they are open from 10am until the beginning of the evening performance.

● Telephone the Box Office — the number can be found either in this book or in the classified or entertainment guides of the press. Seats can be reserved by telephone and paid for either by post or in person, usually within three days.

● Write to the Box Office — enclosing a cheque or postal order and a stamped, addressed envelope giving alternative performance dates if possible.

● Use your credit card — you can telephone the theatre direct quoting your card number, and immediately reserve your seats. You will need to produce your card for identification purposes when collecting your tickets at the theatre.

● Ticket agencies selling West End theatre tickets can be found throughout London and other large cities, some having branches in the larger hotels. These agencies will give you choice of most shows, but some charge an additional booking fee on top of the normal seat prices. It is therefore worth seeking out those agencies from which tickets may be bought for the same price as from the theatre direct. These are indicated in the London Theatre Guide.

The London Theatre Guide

The London Theatre Guide is a fortnightly publication, containing information about theatre productions within the West End. Subscription enquiries should be addressed to:
The Society of West End Theatre, Bedford Chambers, The Piazza, Covent Garden, London WC2.

The Half Price Ticket Booth

Theatre tickets for many West End shows may be bought for half price plus a 75p booking fee from the Leicester Square Ticket Booth. The Booth is open from Monday to Saturday from 12.00 noon for matinee performances and between 2.30pm and 6.30pm for evening performances.

Theatre Gift Tokens

Theatre tokens are now on sale and make the perfect gift. They are available in £1 and £5 units which can be combined to any total value. They come on a presentation card and may be bought and exchanged at most West End Theatre box offices and the Half-Price Ticket Booth, or by post from:

Theatre Gift Tokens, The Society of West End Theatre, Bedford Chambers, The Piazza, Covent Garden, London WC2E 8HQ. (Access, Barclaycard, American Express and Diners' Club cards are welcome) or telephone Tokenline on 01-379 3395.

Senior Citizen's Matinee Scheme

Many theatres offer reduced price tickets for matinees to Senior Citizens. These can be booked in advance either by telephone or in person, or just prior to the performance on presentation of a membership card at the Theatre Box Office. Theatres which operate the scheme are identified in the London Theatre Guide and the West End Theatre Magazine by the symbol R. Membership enquiries should be sent to: Senior Citizen's Matinee Scheme, The Society of West End Theatre, Bedford Chambers, The Piazza, Covent Garden, London WC2E 8HQ.

Student Standby Seats

Unsold seats at many theatres are available cut price to students on production of a student card at the Theatre Box Office just before the performance. Theatres operating this scheme are usually identified by the symbol S in the classified listings.

Sixth Form Standby

An extension of the Student Standby scheme is available to Sixth Formers on presentation of a membership card at the Theatre Box Office. Enquiries should be addressed to:

Sixth Form Standby Scheme, Society of West End Theatre, Bedford Chambers, The Piazza, Covent Garden, London WC2E 8HQ.

Adelphi Theatre

Strand, WC2E 7NH. Map 2

Box Office: 10.00 to 20.00 hrs. **Tel:** 836 7611/2/836 7358 **Bars:** 5 **Cloakroom:** Attendant and Paralok **Seating:** 1,500 **Credit Cards:** Yes **Underground:** Charing Cross **Buses:** 1, 6, 9, 9A, 11, 13, 15, 77, 170, 176.

When seeking a little entertainment in Edwardian times it was fashionable to stroll down the Strand and spend the evening at one of the many theatres, clubs or music halls which abounded. For at the turn of the century, this area around Drury Lane was the heart of lively London. Many of the popular theatres – such as the famous *Gaiety* – have, of course, long since disappeared. But not so *The Adelphi*.

There has been a theatre on the site of the present *Adelphi* since 1806. In 1930 it underwent drastic alterations and today remains much as architect Ernest Schaufelberg designed it. *"The Architect's Journal"* of 3rd December, 1930 noted that " . . . The reconstructed *Adelphi Theatre* is designed with a complete absence of curves. Externally and internally the entire conception is carried out in straight lines and angles . . . the lower half of the walls and fronts of the two circles has been panelled in wood of a deep orange colour, perfectly plain, polished and with no decorative motif whatsoever . . .''

AUDITORIUM PLAN

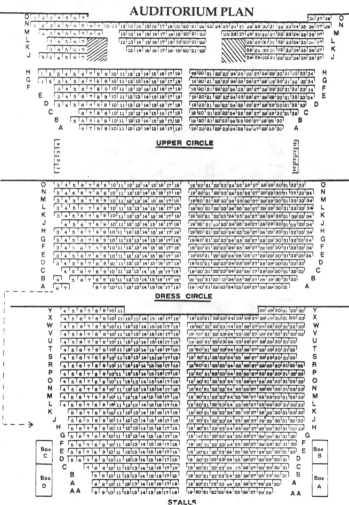

STALLS

Albery Theatre

St. Martin's Lane, WC2N 4AH

Map 2

Box Office: 10.00 to 20.00 hrs. **Tel:** 836 3878 Credit Card Booking: 379 6565 09.00-20.00 hrs **Bars:** 3 **Catering:** No **Cloakroom:** Attendant and Paralok **Seating:** 876 **Credit Cards:** Yes **Underground:** Leicester Square, Piccadilly Circus **Buses: 1, 24, 29, 176.**

Charles Wyndham, manager of *The Criterion Theatre* for twenty-three years, was also the owner of a plot of land between Charing Cross Road and St. Martin's Lane. On the Charing Cross Road side he built the theatre which took his name – and the remainder he planned to sell. However, negotiations fell through and Wyndham decided instead to build another theatre. It was known originally as *The New Theatre* but in 1973 it was changed to *The Albery* – the name, in fact, of the present manager who is himself a direct descendant of Wyndham and his actress wife, Mary Moore.

Albery

The souvenir from the opening night records " . . . on entering the auditorium one is immediately struck with the exquisite lines on which the theatre has been designed, a clear and uninterrupted view of the stage being obtained from literally every part of the theatre . . . the theatre is equipped with all modern and scientific appliances . . . " This is an innovative tradition which continues, for *The Albery* recently became the first theatre in London to introduce electrical flying scenery.

Also unchanged in this elegant Edwardian theatre is the decoration which is in the style of Louis XVI. Either side of the proscenium are models of cupids illustrating peace and music, winter and summer, while extending the French theme, there are panels in the auditorium decorated with portrait medallions of the kings and queens of France.

AUDITORIUM PLAN

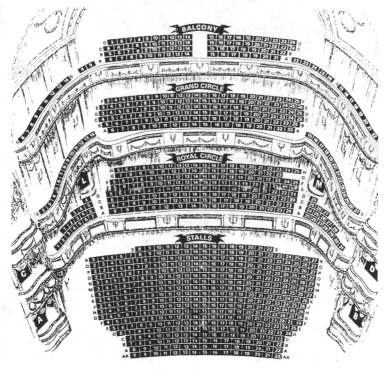

Aldwych Theatre

Aldwych, WC2B 4DF.

Map 2

Box Office: 10.00 to 20.00 hrs. **Tel:** 836 6404 **Bars:** 3 **Cloakroom:** Attendant **Seating:** 1089 **Credit Cards:** Yes **Underground:** Covent Garden, Holborn **Buses:** 1, 4, 6, 9, 11, 13, 15, 55, 68, 77, 170, 171, 172, 176, 188, 239, 501.

At the end of the 19th century when the slums between Drury Lane and Lincoln's Inn were being cleared to make way for two new roads – to be known as The Aldwych and Kingsway – several new theatres were planned. These included two which were to be a "pair" – *The Waldorf* (now *The Strand*) and *The Aldwych*. "*The Era*" of 30th December 1905 comments that " . . . Mr Sprague has not only introduced into his architectural scheme the latest improvements in theatre construction, but has also made certain departures which are all in the right direction. The decorations are in the Georgian style and the general appearance of the interior of the building is pleasing in the extreme. Handsome and ornate it certainly is, but the words that correctly describe the impression conveyed by the first glance around, are cosy and comfortable . . . "

AUDITORIUM PLAN

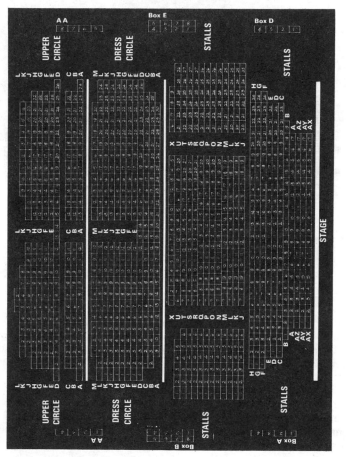

25

Ambassadors Theatre

West Street, WC2H 9ND   **Map 2**

Box Office: 10.00 to 20.00 hrs. **Tel:** 836 6111/836 3212 **Bars:** 3 **Catering:** Yes **Cloakroom:** Attendant and Paralok **Seating:** 460 **Credit Cards:** Yes **Underground:** Leicester Square **Buses:** 1, 14, 19, 22, 24, 29, 38, 176.

On 25th November, 1952 a legend began at *The Ambassadors Theatre*. A thriller – destined to run longer than any other play or musical ever performed in Britain – opened. The play, of course, was Agatha Christie's "The Mousetrap" which, after an incredible run, was transferred to *The St. Martin's Theatre* next door in March 1974.

The Ambassadors was built just before the outbreak of the First World War. It is a welcoming little London theatre with a special air of intimacy all its own. *"The Era"* of 7th June, 1913 recorded that " . . . The general scheme of decoration is Louis XVI . . . " and the original style is much the same today, with ambassadorial crests adorning the auditorium.

The Ambassadors became noted for the staging of revues, and in fact was the first theatre in England to put on an 'intimate revue', a mode of entertainment which was to become so popular.

AUDITORIUM PLAN

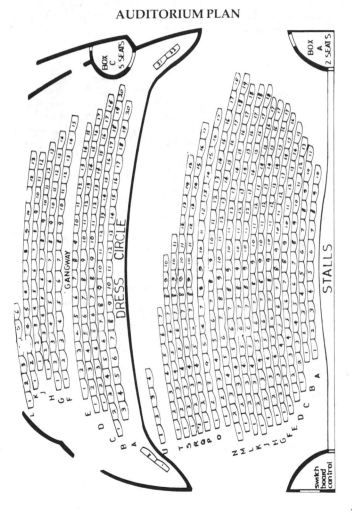

Apollo Theatre

Shaftesbury Avenue, W1V 7HD   **Map 2**

Box Office: 10.00 to 20.00 hrs. **Tel:** 437 2663 **Bars:** 2 **Catering:** Snacks
Cloakroom: Attendant **Seating:** 780 **Credit Cards:** Yes **Underground:**
Piccadilly Circus **Buses:** 14, 19, 22, 38

1887 saw the opening of a new road, which cut through the middle of
Soho and which was soon to become synonymous with entertainment — taking precedence over The Strand as the centre of London's
theatreland. The name of the road was, of course, Shaftesbury Avenue
and one of its first theatres was *The Apollo*.

Apollo

Built in 1901 by Lewen Sharp for owner and manager Henry
Lowenfeld, *The Apollo* has changed very little over the years. The
exterior is in the French Renaissance style and the interior is won-
derfully ornate and elegant in pink, turquoise and gold, adorned with
eagles and statues. Lowenfeld's family estate in Poland had a tribe of
German gipsies and the original badge of the clan — regarded as the
theatre's mascot — can still be seen in the dress circle.

In the early days *The Apollo* concentrated on musicals and for this
reason the name was considered to be particularly appropriate.
Lowenfeld also paid great attention to the orchestra, designing a
special pit and ensuring that each instrument would be heard clearly
and in correct relation to the others.

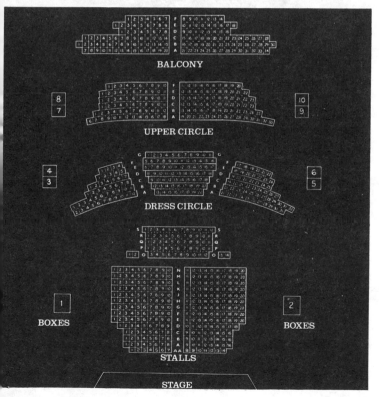

Apollo Victoria Theatre

Wilton Road, SW1 Map 5

Box Office: 10.00 to 20.00 hrs. **Tel:** 630 6262 (10.00 to 22.00) **Party Bookings:** 828 6188 **Bars:** Open to 23.00 **Cloakroom:** Attendant **Seating:** 2572 **Credit Cards:** Yes **Underground:** Victoria.

Built in 1930 as one of the super cinemas of the period, the New Victoria, as it was then called, was "a vigorously modern exterior in line with the finest design of the time".

The interior was the work of Trent and Walmsley Lewis and, in its original colours of blue and green, was a highly successful example of the 'atmospheric' auditorium, giving a striking impression of entering an underwater world.

Now redecorated as the Apollo Victoria in pink, gold and white, the theatre still retains all its decorative features and plasterwork, and the atmosphere is warm and intimate, belying its size.

Apollo Victoria

The theatre, which is a 'listed building', benefits enormously from its original design for both cinema and stage presentations, combining clear, uncluttered sight lines with all the elaborate technical facilities of the West End.

Audiences have always been struck by the spaciousness of the foyer which runs through the building, giving two identical main entrances at Wilton Road and Vauxhall Bridge Road, and with the craftsmenlike detail of beautifully inlaid doors and the numerous witty carved reliefs which, as in medieval buildings, abound in the most unexpected places.

AUDITORIUM PLAN

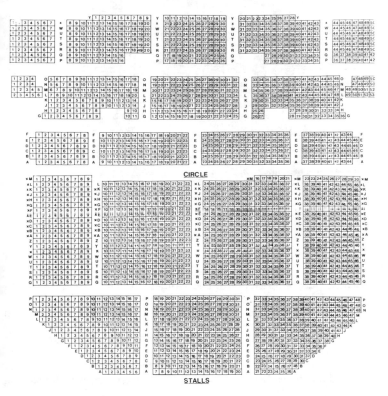

Arts Theatre Club

6/7 Great Newport Street, WC2H 7JA   **Map 2**

Box Office: 10.00 to 20.00 hrs. **Tel:** 836 2132 **Bars:** 1 **Catering:** Restaurant **Cloakroom:** No **Seating:** 340 **Credit Cards:** No **Underground:** Leicester Square **Buses:** 1, 24, 29, 17(

Theatre censorship existed in Tudor times — but in the reign of James I responsibility was placed on the shoulders of the Lord Chamberlain. In 1737, he became the official Licensing Authority for all London theatres (except the Patent theatres), all Royal residences, and also for theatrical societies and clubs — although this latter prerogative was seldom exercised.

As a result of this 'loophole' in the censorship regulations, a number of small theatre clubs grew up in London between the wars for staging experimental productions. *The Arts Theatre Club,* between St. Martin's Lane and Charing Cross Road opened in 1927. Between 1942 and 1953 the Arts Theatre under Alec Clunes developed a 'pocket National Theatre'. In the mid-fifties Peter Hall presented the premiere of 'Waiting for Godot'. In the mid-sixties the R.S.C. presented seasons. In 1967 the Victorian Theatre for children took over the theatre, presenting new plays for children and leasing it at night to long runs of 'Kennedy's Children' and 'Dirty Linen' in the seventies.

AUDITORIUM PLAN

CIRCLE

F	1	2	3	4	5	7	8	9	10	11	12	13	14			
E	1	2	3	4	5	6	7	8	9	10	11	12	13	14	15	16	17
D	1	2	3	4	5	6	7	8	9	10	11	12	13	14	15	16	17
C	1	2	3	4	5	6	7	8	9	10	11	12	13	14	15	16	17
B	1	2	3	4	5	6	7	8	9	10	11	12	13	14	15	16	
A	1	2	3	4	5	6	7	8	9	10	11	12	13	14			

Left side: 7, 6 14, 5 13, 4 12, 3 11, 2 10, 1 9, 8

Right side: 7, 14 6, 13 5, 12 4, 11 3, 10 2, 9 1, 8

STALLS

N	1	2	3	4	5	6	7	8	9	10	11	12	13	14			
M	1	2	3	4	5	6	7	8	9	10	11	12	13	14	15	16	
L	1	2	3	4	5	6	7	8	9	10	11	12	13	14	15	16	17	18
K	1	2	3	4	5	6	7	8	9	10	11	12	13	14	15	16	17	18
J	1	2	3	4	5	6	7	8	9	10	11	12	13	14	15	16	17	18
H	1	2	3	4	5	6	7	8	9	10	11	12	13	14	15	16		
G	1	2	3	4	5	6	7	8	9	10	11	12	13	14	15			
F	1	2	3	4	5	6	7	8	9	10	11	12	13	14	15	16	17	18
E	1	2	3	4	5	6	7	8	9	10	11	12	13	14	15	16	17	18
D	1	2	3	4	5	6	7	8	9	10	11	12	13	14	15	16	17	18
C	1	2	3	4	5	6	7	8	9	10	11	12	13	14	15	16	17	18
B	1	2	3	4	5	6	7	8	9	10	11	12	13	14	15	16	17	
A	1	2	3	4	5	6	7	8	9	10	11	12	13	14				

STAGE

Astoria Theatre

Charing Cross Road, WC2H 0EN   **Map 2**

Box office: 10.00 to 20.00 hrs. **Tel:** 734 4287/8/9 **Bars:** 2 **Catering:** No
Cloakroom: Attendant **Seating:** 820 **Credit Cards:** Yes **Underground:**
Tottenham Court Road, Leicester Square **Buses:** 1, 14, 19, 22, 24, 29,
38, 73, 170.

The Astoria Theatre was originally constructed as a jam factory but
later in the 1930s converted into a cinema that was never particularly
successful. In 1974 it was further converted into a live theatre by
Laurie Marsh in association with Ray Cooney. Between them, they
presented a series of shows at the Astoria, the most successful of
which was "Elvis", running for some 18 months.

Astoria

Laurie Marsh began converting the old "traditional" Astoria Theatre into a cabaret theatre in 1980. It duly opened with the Ray Cooney show "Wild Wild Women" in May 1982. It was reconverted back to its original seating for "Jukebox" in 1983-4, followed by the hit musical "The Hired Man" presented by Andrew Lloyd Webber.

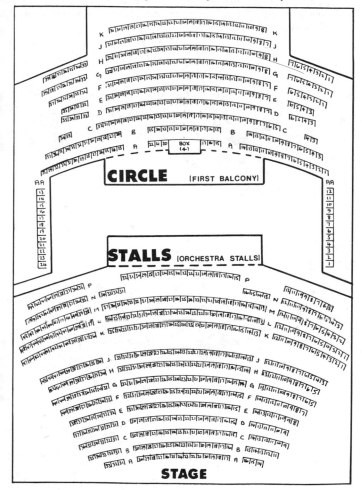

Barbican Centre

Advance Booking for all performances.   **Map 5**
Box Office: 10.00 to 20.00 hrs. **Box Office Tel:** 628 8795/638 8891 **Tel:**
Credit Cards 638 8891 **Recorded information service:** 628 9760-628
2295 **Bars:** 7. Catering: Snacks, Selfservice and Restaurant. **Cloakroom:**
Yes **Underground: Moorgate, Barbican, St. Pauls, Bank. Buses:** 4, 8,
9, 11, 21, 22, 25, 43, 76, 104, 133, 141, 214, 271. For Pedestrians: the
main access is at Silk Street, but overground walkway called The
Podium gives access.

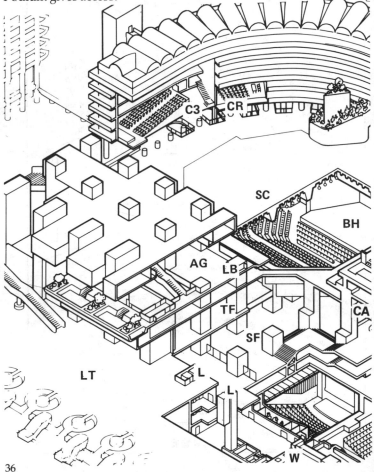

Barbican Centre

"One of the wonders of the modern world" was Queen Elizabeth II's description of the Barbican Centre for Arts and Conferences which she opened on 3 March 1982.

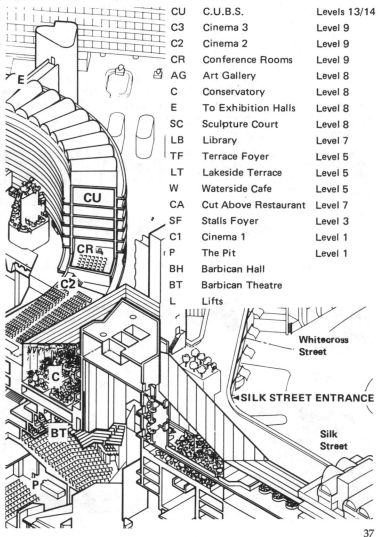

CU	C.U.B.S.	Levels 13/14
C3	Cinema 3	Level 9
C2	Cinema 2	Level 9
CR	Conference Rooms	Level 9
AG	Art Gallery	Level 8
C	Conservatory	Level 8
E	To Exhibition Halls	Level 8
SC	Sculpture Court	Level 8
LB	Library	Level 7
TF	Terrace Foyer	Level 5
LT	Lakeside Terrace	Level 5
W	Waterside Cafe	Level 5
CA	Cut Above Restaurant	Level 7
SF	Stalls Foyer	Level 3
C1	Cinema 1	Level 1
P	The Pit	Level 1
BH	Barbican Hall	
BT	Barbican Theatre	
L	Lifts	

Barbican Theatre

The RSC is built around a core of Associate Artists (actors, directors and designers) who, by working together over long periods with shared ideas, aim to achieve a distinctive style. The Company was formed in 1960 under the leadership of Peter Hall at Stratford-upon-Avon and later that year it took over the Aldwych Theatre as its London headquarters.

The 1166-seat auditorium consists of a raked stalls area and three circles which project forward above each other towards the stage. The stage lies in front of, rather than behind, an arch, and the acting area is the focal point of every seat in the house. The most distant seat is only 65 feet from the front of the stage. Above the stage is a 109-foot double height flytower for scenery storage, believed to be one of the tallest in the world.

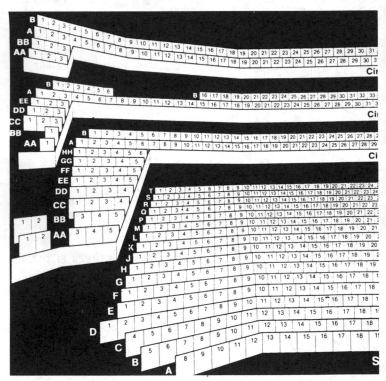

Barbican — The Pit

Complementing the Company's main-stage productions in the Barbican Theatre, the Royal Shakespeare Company presents small-scale productions of Shakespeare, revivals and new plays in The Pit. The Company thus continues its successful policy at the Warehouse in Covent Garden — acting as a London house for transfers from the RSC's small Stratford theatre — The Other Place.

Originally intended as a rehearsal room, The Pit has been adapted to form a flexible auditorium seating around 200 people on three or four sides of the acting area, depending on the design of individual productions. It has no set seating plan.

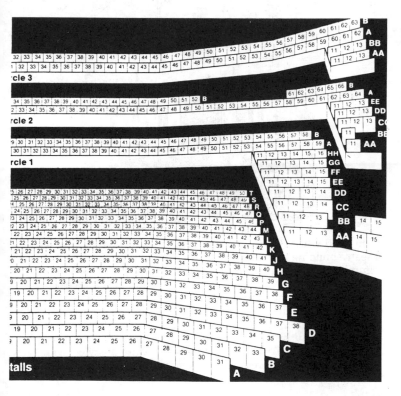

Cambridge Theatre

Earlham Street, WC2 9HU

Box Office: 10.00 to 20.00 hrs. **Tel:** 836 6056 **Bars:** 4 **Catering:** Snacks **Cloakroom:** Attendant **Seating:** 1,273 **Credit Cards:** Yes **Underground:** Covent Garden **Buses:** 1, 14, 19, 22, 24, 29, 38, 176.

In 1930 when *The Cambridge* opened, there was another burst of theatre building going on in London. In the design of *The Cambridge* simplicity was, apparently, the keynote. *"The Stage"* of 4th September, 1930 remarked " . . . The beautiful, if somewhat peculiar decorative scheme appears to be Teutonic, and is strangely reminiscent of the then strange futuristic sets in German films immediately after the war of 1914-1918 . . . " In 1950 the theatre was completely refurbished in red, and a large candelabra and chandeliers were introduced. Today the theatre is a mixture of styles, with a few touches of the thirties remaining – such as the engraved mirrors in one of the bars.

AUDITORIUM PLAN

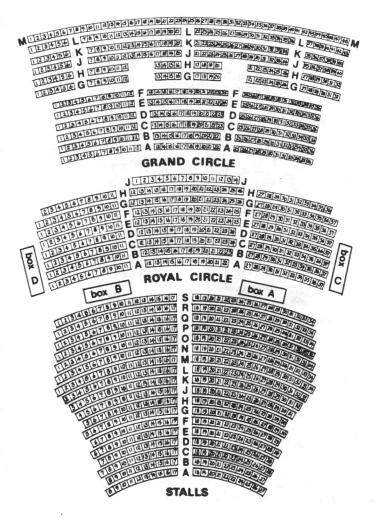

GRAND CIRCLE

ROYAL CIRCLE

STALLS

Comedy Theatre

Panton Street, SW1Y 4DN Map 2

Box Office: 10.00 to 20.00 hrs. **Tel:** 930 2578 **Bars:** 3 **Cloakroom:** Attendant **Seating:** 780 **Credit Cards:** 839 1438 **Underground:** Piccadilly Circus **Buses:** 1, 3, 6, 9, 12, 13, 14, 15, 19, 22, 38, 39, 53, 59, 88, 159, 505, 506.

The architect of *The Comedy* was Thomas Verity – who had the distinction of being one of the first English architects to design in a true French manner. (The French influence on theatre design, especially, was to continue into the early part of the 20th century.) Of his *Comedy Theatre*, "The Era" of 15th October, 1881 remarked " . . . It is Renaissance style richly moulded and finished in white and gold . . . "

Although electric light was to have been installed (as in *The Savoy*, which opened a few days before), the conventional gas system eventually prevailed. In less well-designed auditoria of this period the oxygen-consuming gas burners, together with overcrowding, made conditions extremely uncomfortable. In fact, in 1884 Dr. Angus Smith analysed air taken from the dress circles of various theatres and pronounced it fouler than that found in most sewers! According to *The Era*", however, Verity's work was worthy of praise. It comments on

" . . . abundant room being set apart for each person . . . " and notes that " . . . The pit is open and airy . . . "

Until 1954, when an extensive redecoration scheme took place, *The Comedy* had London's oldest Victorian auditorium. Today it is still a charming little theatre, having an almost cosy 'drawing room' atmosphere – with its wallpaper, pink seating and polished wood doors leading into the shallow dress circle. The corridors are also decorated with attractive costume prints and old theatre bills.

AUDITORIUM PLAN

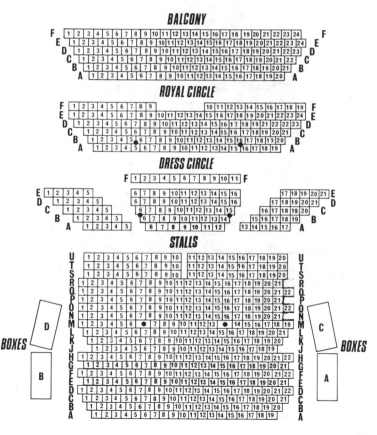

Criterion Theatre

Piccadilly Circus, W1V 9LB **Map 2**

Box Office: 10.00 to 20.00 hrs. **Tel:** 930 3216 Credit Card Booking
09.00-20.00 379 6565 **Bars:** 2 **Catering:** Coffee **Cloakroom:** Paralok
Seating: 602 **Credit Cards:** Yes **Underground:** Piccadilly Circus **Buses:**
6, 9, 12, 13, 14, 15, 19, 22, 25, 38, 39, 53, 59, 88, 159.

In 1873 Spiers and Pond constructed a large restaurant, the Criterion,
overlooking Piccadilly Circus, then known as Regent Circus. In the
initial plans a small concert hall was to be incorporated in the middle of
the building – however, during the construction, it was decided
instead to convert it into a theatre. But this was to be no ordinary
theatre for the designer, Thomas Verity, decided that it should be
underground and even the upper circle had to be reached by
descending stairs. In 1874 the idea was something of a novelty, " . . .

44

Criterion

an underground Temple of Drama into which it was necessary to pump air to save the audience from being asphyxiated . . . "

One of the most delightful features of this charming little theatre is the beautifully preserved Victorian tile work and wall decorations. The auditorium which is pink, beige, soft and warm, manages to combine a quiet elegance with a cosy intimacy – qualities special to so many of the smaller London theatres.

AUDITORIUM PLAN

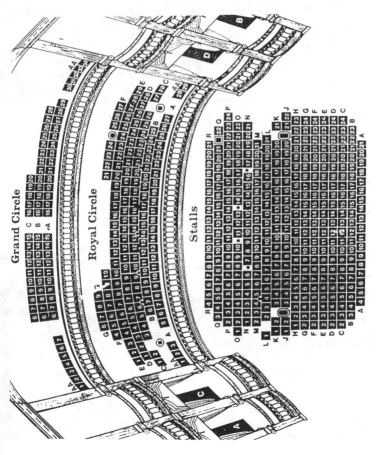

River Thames circa 1640

The City of London and
River Thames circa 1640 – showing
The Globe Theatre.

Donmar Theatre

41 Earlham Street, Covent Garden WC2H 9LD   **Map 2**

Box Office: tel: 836 3028 Credit Card Booking 379 6433 **Bars:** 1 **Catering:** Snacks **Cloakroom:** No **Seating:** 200 **Credit Cards:** Yes **Underground:** Covent Garden **Buses:** 1, 14, 19, 22, 24, 29, 38, 176.

It's easy to pass by *The Warehouse* — in *The Donmar Theatre* in the heart of Covent Garden — without noticing it. You will see no bright lights or grand foyer for this is theatre in the raw! Operated by Omega Projects Ltd. A non-profit registered charity company.

The auditorium is simple — literally a warehouse with seats arranged around the stage area giving it an air of informality. (Seats are not numbered). Seats between 200 and 250.

AUDITORIUM PLAN

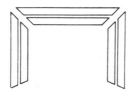

Drury Lane Theatre

Catherine Street, WC2B 5JF   **Map 2**

Box Office: 10.00 to 20.00 hrs. **Tel:** 836 8108 **Bars:** 4 **Catering:** Snacks
Cloakroom: Attendant **Seating:** 2,245 **Credit Cards:** Yes
Underground: Covent Garden, Aldwych **Buses:** 1, 4, 6, 9, 11, 13, 15,
55, 68, 77, 170, 171, 172, 188, 239, 501.

If such a shrine were to be dedicated then *Drury Lane* would surely
become a High Altar of the Theatre, for probably nowhere else is quite
so richly encrusted with its lore.

Since Restoration times four theatres have been housed on the site
of the present theatre. Two were destroyed by fire, one was
demolished and the fourth remains. It would take volumes to describe
the sheer glory of 'The Lane' with its architecture, paintings and
statuary. Because the theatre has always been a mirror of fashion,
styles have changed constantly, being influenced by grandiose
continental themes, heavy Victoriana, Baroque flourishes and
Edwardian imperialism. All are now intrinsically bound together by
time, creating an atmosphere that is sometimes awesome, yet always
welcoming.

The Patent and Charter of Old Drury (a copy of which is on view)
was granted on 25th April, 1662 by King Charles II to Thomas
Killigrew " . . . to erect a company of players consisting of such

Drury Lane

persons as he shall chuse and appoint, and to purchase, builde, or hire at his charge a house or theatre . . . " The King's Company of Players thus became part of the Royal Household and had an allowance of " . . . 10 yards of scarlet cloth and a suitable quantity of lace . . . " The Royal livery is still worn by the theatre footmen and, not unnaturally, many other traditions and ceremonies, not to mention ghosts such as 'the man in grey', still abound at *Drury Lane*.

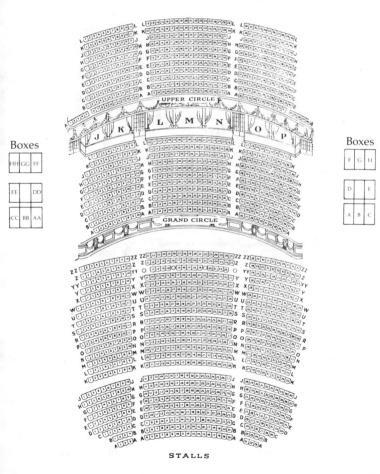

Boxes

STALLS

Duchess Theatre

Catherine Street, WC2B 5LA   **Map 2**

Box Office: 10.00 to 20.00 hrs. **Tel:** 836 8243 **Bars:** 2 **Catering:** No **Cloakroom:** Paralok **Seating:** 474 **Credit Cards:** Yes **Underground:** Covent Garden, Aldwych **Buses:** 1, 4, 6, 9, 11, 13, 15, 55, 68, 77, 170, 171, 172, 188, 239, 501.

1929, the brink of the depression, was an unlikely time to consider building a new theatre and, because of the numerous restrictions imposed, the theatre that was planned in Catherine Street was to be something of a headache for the architect and engineers concerned. But Arthur Gibbons found a brilliant architect in Ewan Barr, whose exterior design for the theatre has been described as 'Modern Tudor Gothic'. It was, however, the interior which was to be the feat of the combined genius of Barr and builders F. G. Minter Ltd. The single circle was designed to be narrower than the stalls, the former being held by steel hangers from girders at roof level. The construction

Duchess

resulted in one of the best planned theatres in London, there being an excellent view from, quite literally, every seat. Today, advanced lighting techniques and a fully equipped cinema projection unit give *The Duchess* a versatility to match the imagination of any director!

J. B. Priestley, as author of "Laburnum Grove", came to the theatre in 1933 and soon after started his long association with the management in which time two more of his plays were produced. His wife Mary Wyndham Lewis redesigned the interior in 1934 at which time a manifesto mentioned that " . . . Mr. Maurice Lambert, the brilliant sculptor, was commissioned to design and execute two great panels, in low bas-relief, for the niches between the proscenium and the dress circle . . . Patrons can see for themselves how well he triumphed and universal admiration has been expressed for his designs of figures holding conventional masks above applauding hands . . . "

AUDITORIUM PLAN

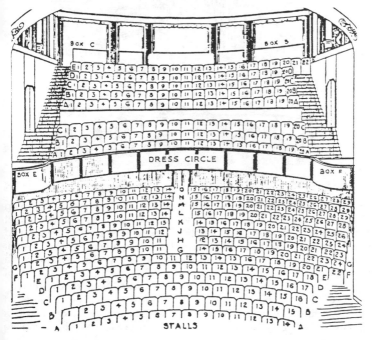

Duke of York's Theatre

St. Martin's Lane, WC2N 4BG

Map 2

Box Office: 10.00 to 20.00 hrs. **Tel:** 836 5122/3 **Bars:** 2 **Catering:** Coffee **Cloakroom:** Attendant **Seating:** 650 **Credit Cards:** Yes **Underground:** Leicester Square **Buses:** 1, 24, 29, 176.

The Duke of York's Theatre was opened on 10th September 1892 with 'The Wedding Eve'. Was built by Frank Wyatt and his wife Violet Melnotte. Initally called The Trafalgar Square, the name was shortened to The Trafalgar in 1894 and in the following year became The Duke of York's in honour of the future King, George V. The theatre has a famous association with J. M. Barrie arising from the production of 'Peter Pan' which opened in this theatre in 1904, and was revived every Christmas until 1915. During the run of the play 'Clouds' in 1979, Capital Radio purchased the freehold of the Duke of York's Theatre. The theatre was then closed down in May 1979 for complete re-furbishment, including a number of pillars from the auditorium, and the installation of a recording studio in the gallary. The theatre then re-opened on 28th February 1980 under the aegis of Capital Radio with the play 'Rose' starring Glenda Jackson.

AUDITORIUM PLAN

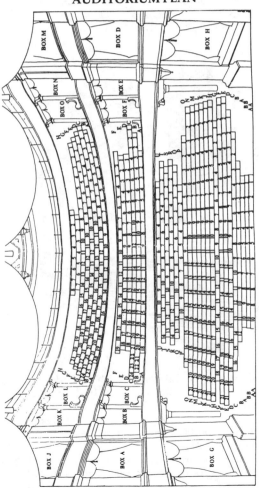

Fortune Theatre

Russell Street, WC2B 5HA

Map 2

Box Office: 10.00 to 20.00 hrs. **Tel:** 836 2238 **Bars:** 2 **Catering** Snacks **Cloakroom:** Yes **Seating:** 432 **Credit Cards:** Yes **Underground:** Covent Garden **Buses:** 1, 1A, 4, 6, 9, 11, 13, 15, 55, 68, 77, 77A, 170, 171, 172, 176, 188, 196, 239, 501, 502, 505, 513.

Way back at the start of the seventeenth century there was a *Fortune Theatre* in Golden Lane, Cripplegate. In 1621 it was burnt down and, after being demolished in 1661, was forgotten for some 300 years. However, Laurence Cowen decided to resurrect the name for his new theatre on the corner of Crown Court in Russell Street, which opened on 8th November, 1924.

The Fortune was the first theatre to be built after the First World War – when money and building materials were scarce. It stands in the

Fortune

heart of the old Covent Garden on the site of the Albion Tavern, frequented by actors and writers in Georgian and Victorian England. Immediately opposite is the stage door and famous colonnade of *The Theatre Royal*, Drury Lane.

What many patrons fail to notice is just how closely *The Fortune* is connected with the Scottish National Church in Crown Court – the passage leading to the church entrance has the theatre above, below and along one side of it! At the time of the construction there was, inevitably, some criticism of this unlikely marriage – although, over-all, there was a wealth of praise for architect Ernest Schaufelberg's work. *"The Era"* of 30th October, 1924 was of the opinion that " . . . the theatre will certainly be one of the most beautiful in London . . . the entrance hall is an exceedingly handsome affair of marble and copper . . " This delightful little foyer remains unchanged, although the auditorium has been renovated and redecorated in white and blue with gold trim and red upholstered seats.

AUDITORIUM PLAN

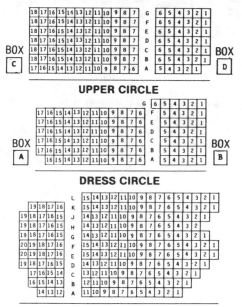

UPPER CIRCLE

DRESS CIRCLE

ORCHESTRA STALLS

Garrick Theatre

Charing Cross Road, WC2H 0HH Map 2

Box Office: 10.00 to 20.00 hrs. **Tel:** 836 4601 **Bars:** 2 **Catering:** No **Cloakroom:** Attendant **Seating:** 675 **Credit Cards:** Yes **Underground:** Leicester Square **Buses:** 1, 24, 29, 176.

In the late 1880s the reputation of the famous theatre architect Phipps was somewhat tarnished after his *Theatre Royal* at Exeter had burned down, causing the loss of some 140 lives. But, although his rival Walter Emden was officially chosen to design W. S. Gilbert's *Garrick Theatre*, Phipps, renowned for his 'clever planning under difficult conditions', was nevertheless consulted. And the conditions at *The Garrick* did indeed prove difficult – an underground river was discovered seeping into the foundations. At this point Gilbert apparently remarked that he couldn't decide whether to continue with the building or lease the fishing rights!

Garrick

Eventually, all the obstacles were overcome and the theatre duly opened on 24th April, 1889. *"The Era"* of 17th April noted that " . . . the auditorium is decorated in the Italian Renaissance style, the ornamental work being in high bold relief . . . the box front of the dress circle tier is divided by groups of cupids supporting shields crowned with laurels, each shield bearing the name of a celebrated author . . ."

The Garrick Theatre today is still heavy with the atmosphere of a Victorian playhouse. It is a richly elegant but friendly little theatre, built under a central dome, graced with magnificent chandeliers and, in the foyer, a copy of a Gainsborough portrait of the celebrated actor Garrick, the original having been lost. In true theatrical tradition there is also a ghost – reputedly that of Arthur Bourchier, a previous manager.

AUDITORIUM PLAN

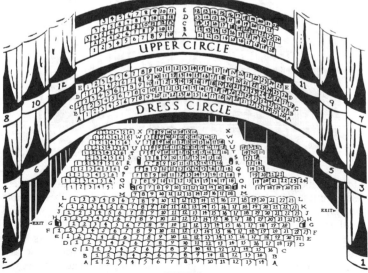

STALLS

Globe Theatre

Shaftesbury Avenue, W1V 7HB Map 2

Box Office: 10.00 to 20.00 hrs. **Tel:** 437 1592 **Bars:** 4 **Catering:** No **Cloakroom:** Attendant **Seating:** 983 **Credit Cards:** Yes **Underground:** Piccadilly Circus **Buses:** 14, 19, 22, 38.

At the turn of the century a considerable number of new theatres were being built in and around London. The architect who was responsible for a great many of them, including most of the elegant little West End theatres which continue to delight, was W. G. R. Sprague.

Sprague was commissioned to design *The Hicks Theatre*, as it was first known, by a group including actor manager Seymour Hicks and Charles Fröhman, the American theatrical manager. The theatre, was opened in 1906.

Globe

Sprague, like several other architects of his time, had a fondness for French themes. (It is interesting to note here that it was Sprague who, in fact, designed *The Edward VII Theatre* in Paris). And, of course, the Monarch's own affection for France possibly had some effect on the fashion of the day. In any event, much of the decorative style of *The Globe* is in the manner of Louis XVI although it must be said that the overall picture also relies on Baroque and Georgian influences.

AUDITORIUM PLAN

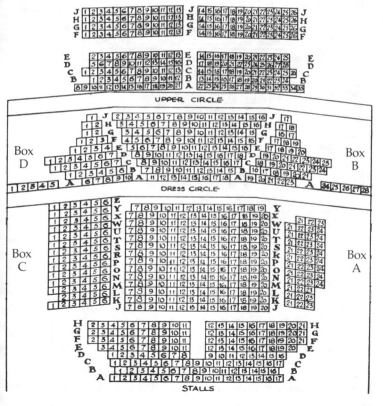

Haymarket, Theatre Royal

Haymarket, SW1Y 4HT.

Map 4

Box Office: 10.00 to 20.00 hrs. **Tel:** 930 9832 **Bars:** 3 **Catering:** No **Cloakroom:** Attendant **Seating:** 906 **Credit Cards: Underground:** Piccadilly Circus, Charing Cross **Buses:** 6, 9, 12, 13, 14, 15, 19, 22, 25, 38, 39, 53, 59, 88, 159.

In the first quarter of the 18th century, only two theatres in London — *Drury Lane* and *Covent Garden,* held the necessary Patent allowing them to open to the public. For many years the "Little Theatre in the Hay" fought the legislation and put on entertainment under various guises. Finally, however, the Patent was obtained through the Duke of York — brother of King George III — and granted to Samuel Foote. *The Theatre Royal* (as it became) was then officially in business — although it was only allowed to open between 14th May and 14th September when the other two charter houses were closed.

In 1821, at a time when much of London was being restyled at the wish of the Prince Regent, the famous architect John Nash was commissioned to redesign the theatre.

Throughout the 19th century various alterations took place, the proscenium being widened and gas lighting introduced —the theatre was, in fact, the last to be lit by candles. Around 1879, the eminent architect Phipps exerted a French influence when he attempted to emulate the interior of Victor Louis' *Grand Théâtre de Bordeaux*. Today, the auditorium with its ornate decor, gilding and ceiling paintings, remains gracious, elegant and decidedly regal.

AUDITORIUM PLAN

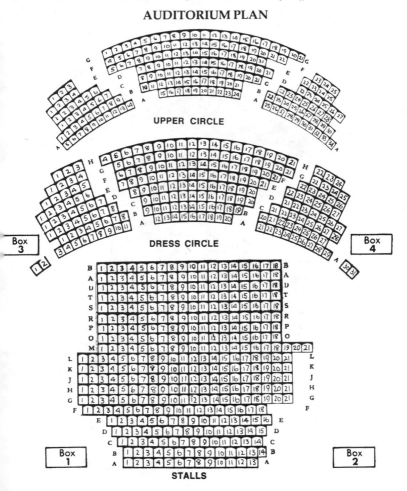

61

Her Majesty's Theatre

Haymarket, SW1Y 4QR
Map 4

Box Office: 10.00 to 20.00 hrs. **Tel:** 930 6606 **Bars:** 3 **Catering:** Coffee **Cloakroom:** Attendant **Seating:** 1,209 **Credit Cards:** Yes **Underground:** Piccadilly Circus **Buses:** 3, 6, 9, 12, 13, 14, 15, 19, 22, 38, 39, 53, 59, 88, 159, 505, 506.

The site of *Her Majesty's* has had theatrical associations since 1705, when the first of the four theatres was built by Sir John Vanbrugh, who described the location as being " . . . the second stableyard going up the Hay-Market . . . " The second theatre, known as *The King's* until 1837, when it became *Her Majesty's*, was the home of Italian opera. It was the largest and most expensive theatre in England and one of the most magnificent and fashionable in the world.

Her Majesty's

The present theatre, built by the famous actor manager Beerbohm Tree, opened in 1897. A contemporary manifesto stated that " . . . the style adopted for the auditorium of the theatre is Louis XIV. There are private boxes on each of the tiers adjoining the proscenium and separated from it and other parts of the auditorium by marble columns . . . The whole of the theatre and annexes are lighted by Electric Light . . . Hanging from the ceiling is a cut glass and brass electrolier . . . " Because of its exceptionally good acoustics, the theatre today is as popular with actors as with audiences. Outside, there still stands the arcade which was designed by Nash and Repton and completed in 1818 – while inside, the predominantly red auditorium with its large stage and fine ceiling paintings, remains as resplendent and dignified as ever.

AUDITORIUM PLAN

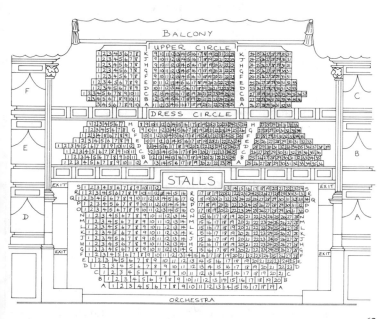

THE
LAURENCE OLIVIER
AWARDS.

In 1984 the Society of West End Theatre Awards were renamed The Laurence Olivier Awards in honour of Britain's most revered actor. First presented in 1976, the Awards are recognised as one of the most prestigious the theatre world can bestow on the actors, actresses, dancers, singers, playwrights, composers, directors and designers whose talents have established London's West End as the theatre centre of the world.

The three adjudicating Panels — Theatre, Opera and Dance are unique in the fact that they not only include people connected with the performing arts chosen for their knowledge and professional experience, but also, very importantly, members of the general public who enjoy going to the theatre regularly and have a wide and varied taste.

This is just one of the many activities organised by the Society of West End Theatre. For further information please turn to page 6.

Olivier

THE
LAURENCE
OLIVIER
AWARDS

THE LONDON THEATRE. ACT ON IT

London Coliseum

Home of
English National Opera

St. Martin's Lane, WC2N 4ES.

Map 2

Box Office: 10.00 to 20.00 hrs. **Tel:** 836 3161 Credit Card Booking:
240 5258 **Bars:** 5 **Catering:** Snacks and salads **Cloakroom:** Attendant
and Paralok **Seating:** 2358 **Credit Cards:** Yes **Underground:** Leicester
Square, Charing Cross, Embankment **Buses:** 1, 3, 6, 9, 11, 12, 13, 15,
23, 24, 29, 53, 77, 77a, 88, 159, 170, 172, 176, 500 all stop nearby.

An exquisitely furnished mobile lounge, designed to transport Royal
guests to their box, lifts to carry audiences to the upper parts of the
theatre, foyer facilities for typing messages and sending telegrams . . .
these were just a few of the innovations which impressed Londoners
in 1904 when Oswald Stoll opened his *London Coliseum*.

As the name implies, the theatre was designed on Romanesque
lines. Grandiose and broad sweeping, complete with Roman chariots,

London Coliseum

granite columns and arches – the sheer splendour remains today. Yet despite the vastness there is a certain warmth and intimacy, typified perhaps in the unusual stalls – level boxes at the back of the auditorium. (There are, of course, conventional boxes at all other levels.)

The globe on the top of the building was designed to revolve but it was deemed illegal and Stoll was obliged to fix it in a stationary

AUDITORIUM PLAN

London Coliseum

position. However, he was able to incorporate flashing electric lights which gave the illusion of movement and this remains a famous feature of the London skyline. In the sixties Sadler's Wells Opera, now English National Opera, made *The Coliseum* their West End home.

International ballet companies also perform for short summer seasons.

The opera season runs from August to May.

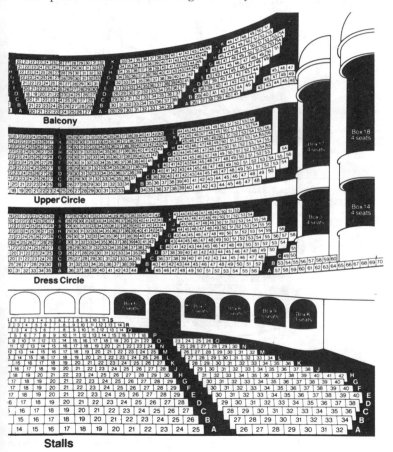

Balcony

Upper Circle

Dress Circle

Stalls

Box 18 4 seats

Box 14 4 seats

London Palladium Theatre

Argyll Street, W1A 3AB **Map 1**

Box Office: 10.00 to 20.00 hrs. **Tel:** 437 7373/437 2055 **Bars:** 5 **Catering:** Snacks **Cloakroom:** Attendant **Seating:** 2,317 **Credit Cards:** Yes **Underground:** Oxford Circus **Buses:** 1, 3, 6, 7, 8, 12, 13, 15, 25, 39, 53, 59, 88, 93.

On Sunday evenings in the sixties Britain switched on to "Sunday Night At The London Palladium" – the variety show which became almost as much of an institution as the Sunday roast itself!

The theatre has, in fact, been associated with variety for many years, while the site on which it is built has been connected with entertainment for over a century.

London Palladium

In 1871, Frederick Hengler acquired a lease on the original property and staged his successful "Hengler's Grand Cirque" – eventually being superseded by the *National Skating Palace*. Efforts were later made to resurrect the circus, but by then the public's imagination had been caught by the more breathtaking spectaculars at the new *London Hippodrome*.

AUDITORIUM PLAN

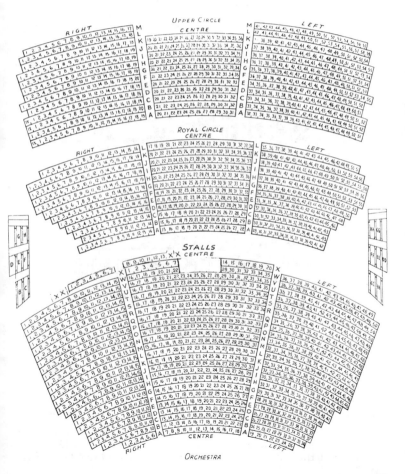

Lyric Theatre

Shaftesbury Avenue, W1V 8ES   Map 2

Box Office: 10.00 to 20.00 hrs. **Tel:** 437 3686 **Bars:** 3 **Catering:** Snacks **Cloakroom:** Attendant **Seating:** 948 **Credit Cards:** Yes **Underground:** Piccadilly Circus **Buses:** 14, 19, 22, 38.

The last years of the 19th century saw great activity in the fast developing areas around the new Shaftesbury Avenue. Undoubtedly there were fortunes to be made and one man who had the key to theatreland success was Henry J. Leslie, builder of *The Lyric Theatre*.

When everyone else was losing heart, Leslie purchased an interest in the initially unsuccessful comic opera "Dorothy" which, after opening at the old *Gaiety Theatre*, had transferred to *The Prince of Wales*.

Lyric

Leslie effected a few changes and soon "Dorothy" started to flourish. He then decided to transfer the show to his own new theatre when it opened, reputedly ending up with a tidy £100,000 profit in his pocket!

In 1933 Michael Rosenauer completely refurbished the theatre leaving on it the unmistakeable stamp of the thirties.

AUDITORIUM PLAN

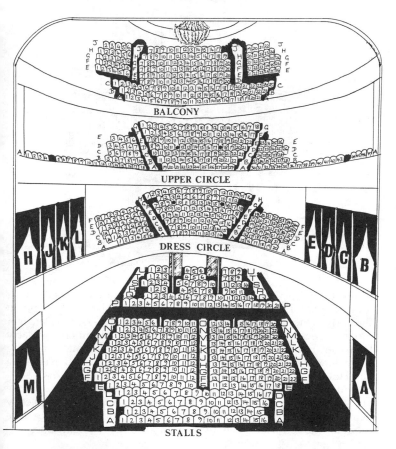

May Fair Theatre

Stratton Street, W1X 5FD

Map 3

Box Office: 10.00 to 20.00 hrs. **Tel:** 629 3036 **Bars and Catering:** Use of hotel facilities **Cloakroom:** Attendant **Seating:** 310 **Credit Cards:** Yes **Underground:** Green Park **Buses:** 9, 14, 19, 22, 25, 38.

In the 1930s the Candlelight Room at the Mayfair Hotel was famous for its Big Band Broadcasting with Ambrose and Harry Roy — but in the early sixties all was transformed when the owners, the Danziger brothers decided to convert it into a theatre. In a radio interview Harry Danziger remarked that it would be ". . . . a unique crowning achievement for the entertainment centre we have created in the May Fair Hotel. . ."

And indeed it was, but as the opening programme states ". . . . the task was far from simple . . . " The ballroom had to be completely demolished along with sections of two floors of bedrooms, to make room for the 26ft wide stage, fly tower and scenery hanging lines.

May Fair

Today, the smart little *Mayfair Theatre* is magnificently equipped for staging live productions of all kinds. It also has first-class audio/visual facilities and an extremely versatile auditorium, which can be altered in various ways to make four different kinds of stage. The seats are removable and raked to give excellent sight lines from all parts of the theatre, and the acoustics are superb – the result of the hotel's requirement for the theatre to have effective soundproofing and insulation. *Mayfair* audiences can, of course, also take advantage of the hotel's many amenities – restaurants, bars and lounges – and enjoy an entire evening's entertainment under one roof.

AUDITORIUM PLAN

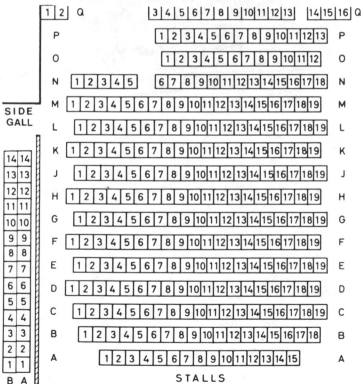

Mermaid Theatre

Puddledock, Blackfriars, EC4V 3DB Map 5

Box Office: 10.00 to 20.00 hrs. **Tel:** 236 5568 **Bar:** 2 **Catering:** Snacks and Restaurant **Cloakroom:** Yes **Seating:** 610 **Credit Cards:** Yes **Underground:** Blackfriars **Buses:** 89, 95, 98, 133.

The Mermaid Theatre is a dream which came true. Lord Bernard Miles and his wife Josephine had always wanted to build their own Elizabethan-style theatre, and in 1945, when they moved to St. John's Wood, the seed was already sown. There, in their own back garden, was a large wooden building (previously a school classroom) which was destined to become the first *Mermaid Theatre,* opening on 9th September, 1951.

In 1952, when Sir Leslie Boyce, the Lord Mayor of London visited *The Mermaid,* he suggested that, during the forthcoming Coronation celebrations, the theatre should 'move' down to the City. So, for a 13-week season the company performed on the Piazza inside the Royal Exchange. From then on it seemed that *The Mermaid* belonged to the City and a permanent home was eventually chosen at Puddledock, immediately opposite Bankside, the site of Shakespeare's old *Globe Theatre.* The new theatre, built within the remains of a blitzed warehouse, was designed with a steeply-raked auditorium and an open stage. On the opening day 4-year old Caroline Hawkins, daughter of actor Jack Hawkins, became a living mermaid and was rowed up the Thames to be delivered into the arms of Lord Mayor, Sir Harold Gillett. The opening production on the 29th May, 1959 was "Lock Up Your Daughters". Since then patrons have been entertained with all kinds of classical and modern drama, revue and pantomime. *The Mermaid* was then closed in 1979 and after extensive modernisation, re-opened in 1981. There are now two foyer bars, a coffee bar and a restaurant overlooking the River Thames. The auditorium and stage areas have been enlarged.

The Mermaid is very much more than a theatre — it is a fountain-head of creativity. In addition to the theatre itself, there is the Molecule Club for schoolchildren between the ages of 7 and 14, the brainchild of Lord Bernard Miles' wife Josephine. Her ingenious idea was to use all the facilities of *The Mermaid* to make learning more fun. Science was the ideal subject to bring to life — not only because to many children it is 'difficult' and 'boring' but also because it lends itself so readily to high drama.

AUDITORIUM PLAN

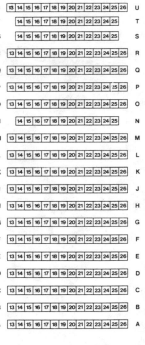

National Theatre

South Bank, SE1 9PX   Map 4

Box Office: 10.00 to 20.00 hrs. **Tel:** 928 2252, 24-hrs. Recorded Tel. booking information: 928 8126 **Credit Card Bookings:** 928 5933 **Bars** 7 **Catering:** Restaurant, last orders 23.00 hrs. **Tel:** 928 2033 Ext. 228. 5 Buffet Bars **Cloakroom:** Attendant **Seating:** See text for each theatre. **Credit Cards:** Yes **Underground:** Waterloo **Buses:** 1, 4, 68, 171, 176, 188, 239, 501, 502, 513. **Car Park:** 08.00 to 02.00, except Sunday.

Details on the many activities and amenities are contained in a pamphlet available from the theatre.

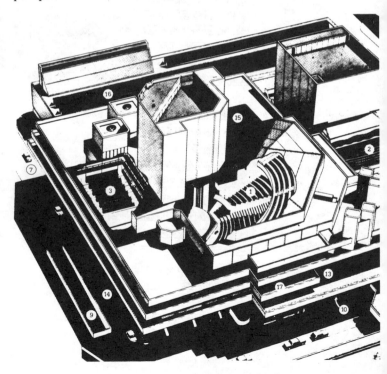

National Theatre

The National Theatre is a great building in every sense. Architect Sir Denys Lasdun incorporated not only **three auditoria** but **eight bars** and a **restaurant** plus modern workshops, paint rooms, wardrobes, property shops, rehearsal rooms and advanced technical facilities, the like of which had never been seen in a British theatre — where backstage, cramped and difficult conditions were all too often the norm.

The concept of Britain's National Theatre is an equally vast one ". . . to do for audiences, artistes, authors, the theatre, arts and country as a whole (socially and culturally) what no other playhouse in Britain can do or could ever hope to do . . . " is the way it has been summarised in the Theatre's Guide. Director Sir Peter Hall's dream of creating not merely a theatre centre but a social centre is also being seen to be coming true, for the atmosphere at *The National Theatre* welcomes everyone.

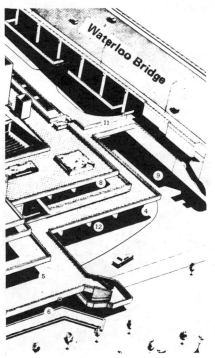

1. Olivier Theatre

2. Lyttelton Theatre

3. Cottesloe Theatre

4. Box Office

5. Terrace entrance, Olivier information desk, cloakroom

6. Main entrance, Lyttelton information desk, cloakroom

7. Cottesloe entrance

8. Lyttelton buffet

9. Car park entrances

10. Restaurant

11. Exits to Waterloo station

12. Lyttelton bookshop

13. Olivier bookshop

14. Stage door

15. Dressing rooms

16. Workshops

17. Olivier buffet

National Theatre/Olivier

There are daily conducted tours of the building (except Sunday) including the workshops and backstage areas. Walk through this amazing complex and, in addition to theatregoers of all ages, you will see visitors and Londoners alike strolling through the spacious foyers; meeting friends; enjoying a drink or a meal; browsing through bookstalls; listening to impromptu music in the foyers; or simply standing on one of the terraces and marvelling at the continuous pageant of craft flowing past the magnificent backdrop of the City on the other side of the water.

Each of Lasdun's theatres is totally different in design and adaptable enough to meet all kinds of dramatic requirements, thus offering enormous scope for both directors and actors. For audiences, too, *The National Theatre* promotes new levels of discovery and enjoyment. The designers have, quite literally, set the stages for much closer communication between actor and audience. Acoustics and sight

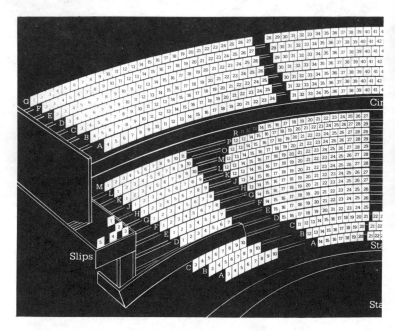

lines in all three theatres are first class, ensuring that every seat is a good one and, incidentally, a reasonably priced one. A high proportion of seats are offered daily at considerably less than one would expect to pay at most West End theatres. The modern facilities at *The National Theatre* also mean that it is easier to cater for a constantly changing repertoire, guaranteeing that at least once a month most tastes can be accommodated!

The theatre, named after actor Sir Laurence Olivier, who was also the first Director of *The National* during its years at *The Old Vic*, is the centre of the complex. It can accommodate 1,160 people in its fan-shaped auditorium and dispenses with the conventional proscenium arch and safety curtain. *The Olivier* can serve dramatists of every period and theatre of every sort, and in spite of its size, has a concentrated intimacy. No seat is far from the actor's point of command and the seats match his effective span of vision, thus adding a new relationship between actor and audience.

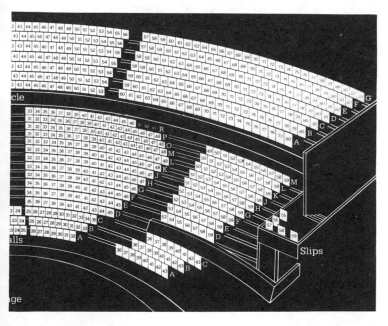

National Theatre/Cottesloe

The Cottesloe is the smallest, barest and most flexible of *The National Theatre* houses. It is a dark-walled rectangular space capable of accommodating up to 400 people if necessary. The seating can be removed and the stage can be used in any way, for any kind of production, from classical staging to experimental theatre.

On three sides of the room are two tiers of pillared galleries — reminiscent of the inn yards which preceded Shakespearean stages. The theatre is named after Lord Cottesloe, Chairman of the South Bank Board (the body for the construction of *The National Theatre)* and a former Chairman of the Arts Council. (No set seating plan).

AUDITORIUM PLAN

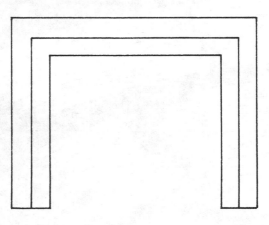

National Theatre/Lyttelton

The Lyttelton is a proscenium theatre which can hold 890 people. As elsewhere in *The National Theatre* the walls are roughly-finished shuttered concrete to promote efficient acoustics. The proscenium is adaptable and it is possible to make an open end-stage effect, while a down-stage lift can create a fore-stage or an orchestra pit for up to 20 musicians.

Complete sets can also be prepared behind soundproof doors ready to slide onto the stage. The theatre is named after Oliver Lyttelton, Viscount Chandos, whose parents were among the earliest campaigners for *The National Theatre* and who was himself its first Chairman from 1962 to 1971.

AUDITORIUM PLAN

New London Theatre

Parker Street, Drury Lane, WC2B 5PW. **Map 2**

Box Office: 10.00 to 19.45 hrs. **Tel:** 405 0072 **Bars:** 2 **Catering:** By arrangement **Cloakroom:** Attendant **Seating:** 907 **Underground:** Covent Garden, Holburn **Buses:** 1, 8, 14, 19, 22, 24, 25, 29, 38, 73, 176.

The New London Theatre, which has been both a conventional theatre and a conference centre in its time.

The site of *The New London* at 167 Drury Lane has held licensed premises since the reign of Elizabeth I. Nell Gwynn, who lived nearby, was associated with the Mogul Tavern of the 17th century, which eventually developed into the Music Hall known to Londoners as "Old Mo". In 1910 it was completely rebuilt and remained the home of music hall, French revue and touring revues until its closure in 1919 when it was acquired by the partnership of Laurillard and Grossmith who redecorated it, as *"The Era"* of 28th October noted, " . . . based entirely on the old French gardens of the transitional period between Louis XIV and Louis XV . . . " It was renamed *The Winter Garden Theatre*, which it remained until its closure in 1959. The building was finally demolished in 1965 and rebuilt in 1971/72 as a complex incorporating a theatre, restaurant, flats, showroom and underground car park. The press release at the time remarked that " . . . *The New London* is a theatre of the future. It is a theatre that moves: stage, seats, lights – even the walls can be made to change position . . . " It is indeed an extremely versatile theatre and can adapt from 'proscenium' to 'theatre-in-the-round' literally at the flick of a switch. Despite its historical foundations, *The New London* is ultra modern in design with a spacious brown and beige auditorium, behind which is the 2,400 square foot foyer with its large glass window, bars and comfortable lounge areas.

No seating plan for this theatre as the seating changes from production to production.

AUDITORIUM PLAN

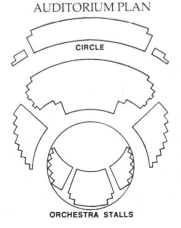

Open Air Theatre

Inner Circle, Regent's park, NW1 4NP   **Map 5**

Box Office: 10.00 to 20.00 hrs. during season: June, July, August, May 10.00 to 17.00 hrs. **Tel:** 486 2431 **Bar:** 1 **Catering:** Cold buffet and Barbecue. Inclusive price (ticket and food) for parties only by prior arrangement. Picnickers welcome. **Cloakroom:** No **Seating:** 1,187 plus 60 on grass **Credit Cards:** Yes **Underground:** Baker Street **Buses:** 1, 2, 2B, 13, 18, 27, 30, 74, 113, 159, 176.

Take a delightful woodland setting, a gentle summer's evening and a fine company of players and you have the magic ingredients which go to make a visit to London's unique *Open Air Theatre* so enjoyable. The idea of staging plays in the park was initiated by Ben Greet whose Woodland Players used to entertain audiences in Edwardian times. In 1932, Sydney Carroll resurrected the tradition, with a few exceptions during the war years. Three productions are now presented in repertory each summer, two of which are the works of Shakespeare.

1975 saw the opening of a new auditorium complex comprising an upper and lower tier — replacing the rows of deck chairs and wooden seats with room beneath for catering facilities. These include a cold buffet service, barbecue and large bar, famous for its cocktail specialities — such as 'Puck's Fizz' and heart-warming mulled wine.

Open Air

The New Shakespeare Company was formed in 1962 under the managing directorship of David Conville, who remains enthusiastically in control today. After the season at Regent's Park his company spends the rest of the year on tour at home and abroad. 'In 1982 the Theatre celebrated its Golden Jubilee and was visited by Her Majesty, the Queen and His Royal Highness, the Duke of Edinburgh.'

AUDITORIUM PLAN

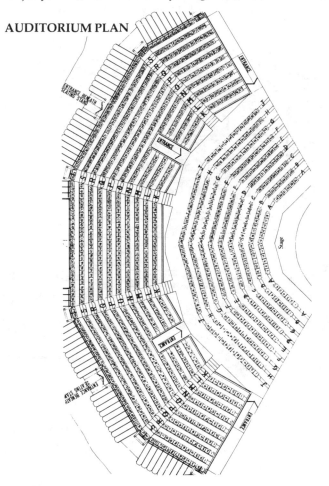

Palace Theatre

Shaftesbury Avenue, W1A 4AF   Map 2

Box Office: 10.00 to 20.00 hrs. **Tel:** 437 6834 **Bars:** 5 **Catering:** Snacks **Cloakroom:** Attendant **Seating:** 1,480 **Credit Cards:** Yes **Underground:** Leicester Square **Buses:** 1, 14, 19, 22, 24, 29, 38, 176.

The Royal English Opera House (as *The Palace* was first known) opened its doors on 31st January, 1891 with "Ivanhoe", a romantic opera by Arthur Sullivan. English audiences, however, failed to support this and the several other offerings which swiftly followed, and Richard D'Oyly Carte's dream of an English Opera House finally faded in 1892 when the theatre became *The Palace Theatre of Varieties*.

Palace

The walls and staircases are resplendent in an extravagance of alabaster veined marble and the ceilings decorated with onyx plaster strapwork. Today, the auditorium is still heavily and sumptuously Victorian — much of D'Oyly Carte's original style of decor remaining. The Theatre is now open between 11.00 a.m. and 3.00 p.m. daily, in addition to normal theatre opening hours. We now serve meals in the stalls bar and provide live entertainment and have a gallery which carries contemporary exhibitions.

AUDITORIUM PLAN

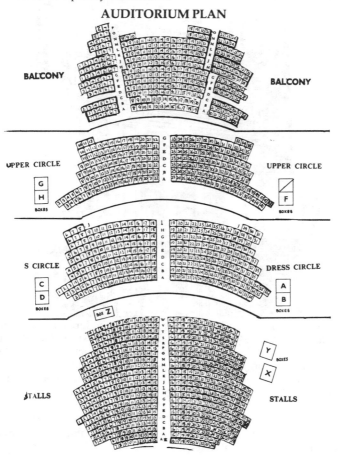

Phoenix Theatre

Charing Cross Road, WC2H 0JP Map 2

Box Office: 10.00 to 20.00 hrs. **Tel:** 836 2294 **Bars:** 4 **Catering:** Coffee and sandwiches **Cloakroom:** Attendant and Paralok **Seating:** 1,000 **Credit Cards:** Yes **Underground:**Tottenham Court Road **Buses:** 1, 14, 19, 22, 24, 29, 38, 176.

For 'The Master', Noel Coward and his beloved Gertrude Lawrence, *The Phoenix* was to be 'their' theatre – in which they starred together on a number of occasions in Coward's own productions. Their first appearance was on the theatre's opening night, in "Private Lives", which Coward had written in about four days while recuperating from a bout of 'flu in Shanghai. His biographer, Cole Lesley remarks that " . . . 'Private Lives' was deck'd in a glorious sheen of success before it started and in addition it was chosen to open Sidney (later Lord) Bernstein's *Phoenix Theatre*, a smart new ornament to London's theatreland, and an event in itself . . . "

Phoenix Theatre

Although it has been redecorated since, the theatre with its wood panelling, red seating and elegant chandelier, retains that delightfully intimate and stylish atmosphere typical of such theatres of the thirties. In 1969, Noel Coward opened the bar which is named after him. In another of the theatre's bars are some famous Punch cartoonists' original interpretations on a theme of 'the rising of the Phoenix'.

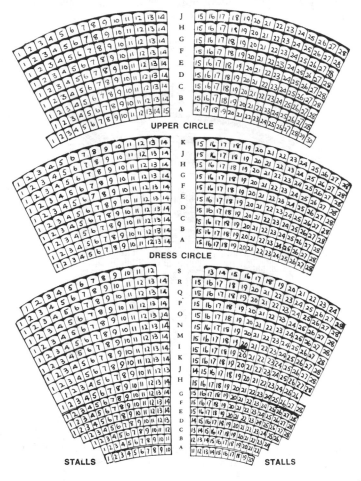

UPPER CIRCLE

DRESS CIRCLE

STALLS   STALLS

Piccadilly Theatre

Denman Street, W1V 8DY. Map 1

Box Office: 10.00 to 20.00 hrs. **Tel;** 437 4506 Credit Card Booking: 379 6565, 09.00 - 20.00 **Bars:** 4 **Catering:** Buffet **Cloakroom:** Attendant and Paralok **Seating:** 1128 **Underground:** Piccadilly Circus **Buses:** 3, 6, 9, 13, 14, 15, 19, 22, 25, 38, 39, 53, 59, 88, 159.

Victorian and Edwardian times, the heydays of British theatre building, inevitably nurtured a certain breed of architect who specialised in theatre design – Frank Matcham, William Sprague and Bertie Crewe, to name but a few. Although this golden age had largely diminished by the late twenties, Bertie Crewe still brought all his flair and expertise to the designing of *The Piccadilly Theatre*.

Piccadilly

The area chosen for impresario Edward Laurillard's new theatre was covered by run-down stables but by 1928 they had been replaced by a handsome building of white Portland stone. The original interior design was carried out by Marc-Henri but has since been altered, the modern amenities now including air conditioning and well appointed bars.

AUDITORIUM PLAN

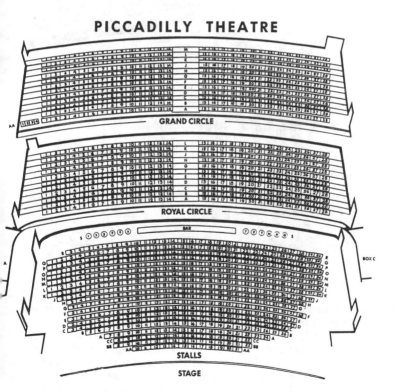

91

Prince Edward Theatre

Old Compton Street, W1V 6HS Map 2

Box Office: 10.00 to 20.00 hrs. **Tel:** 437 6877 **Bars:** 4 **Catering:** No
Cloakroom: Paralok **Seating:** 1,666 **Credit Cards:** Yes **Underground:**
Leicester Square, Piccadilly Circus, Tottenham Court Road **Buses:** 1,
14, 19, 22, 24, 29, 38.

Designed by Edward A. Stone, *The Prince Edward* was the first of a
spate of theatres to be constructed in the thirties. Within five years,
however, it was converted into a cabaret-restaurant and at one point
The London Casino (as it was now known), was reputed to be taking
between £6,000 and £7,000 a week – more than any other place of
entertainment in London! In 1946 it became a theatre once more – until
1954, when after suitable conversions, the big screen Cinerama
arrived. In 1974, under Bernard Delfont's direction, the theatre was
converted into a dual purpose film and theatre centre.

Prince Edward

In 1978 Andrew Lloyd Webber and Tim Rice's hit musical "Evita" brought visitors and residents alike flocking to *The Prince Edward*.

AUDITORIUM PLAN

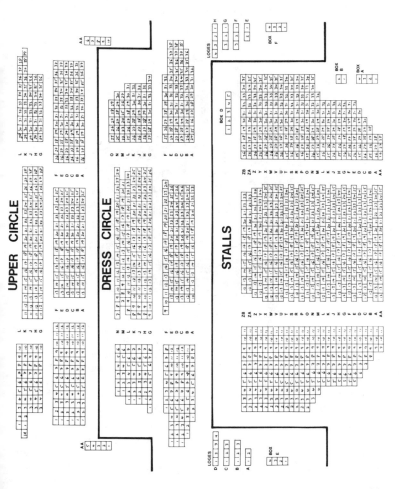

Prince of Wales Theatre

Coventry Street, W1V 8AS

Map 2

Box Office: 10.00 to 20.00 hrs. **Tel:** 930 8681 **Bars:** 3 **Catering:** No **Cloakroom:** Paralok **Seating:** 1,122 **Credit Cards:** Yes **Underground:** Piccadilly Circus **Buses:** 3, 6, 9, 12, 13, 14, 15, 19, 22, 25, 38, 39, 53, 59, 88, 159.

The Prince of Wales, now under the direction of Lord Delfont and a member of the now FIRST LEISURE CORPORATION PLC, is essentially a happy theatre, synonymous with good family entertainment and, of course, famous for its numerous television broadcasts. Walking into the spacious auditorium one can almost hear the spontaneous laughter and enthusiastic applause which have echoed round the rafters on so many glorious occasions.

Originally known as *The Prince's,* the theatre was built by actor manager Edgar Bruce in 1884. *"The Era"* of the 12th January mentions that " . . . the general tone of the decorations is navy, white, cream colour and gold, the gilding being in large masses . . . the audience to the stalls, after leaving the vestibule, descend by a spacious staircase through a foyer which is decorated and fitted up in the Moorish style and under the vestibule is a circular room, also in the Moorish style, for smoking, having a grotto constructed under the street . . .''

But in 1936 all that was to change. Robert Cromie redesigned *The Prince of Wales* (the name changed in 1886) in a style typical of the era – with sweeping curves and almost stark simplicity. And for anyone who has had to employ football scrum techniques in order to get a drink at some of the smaller theatre bars, there is good news – those at *The Prince of Wales* have been constructed on a grand scale!

AUDITORIUM PLAN

DRESS CIRCLE

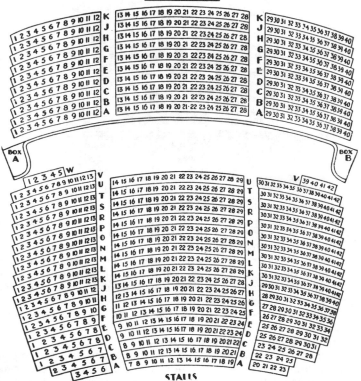

STALLS

Queen's Theatre

Shaftesbury Avenue, W1V 8BA   Map 2

Box Office: 10.00 to 20.00 hrs. **Tel:** 734 1166 **Bars:** 2 **Catering:** Coffee
Cloakroom: Attendant **Seating:** 979 **Credit Cards:** Yes **Underground:**
Piccadilly Circus **Buses:** 14, 19, 22, 38.

"He is after a knighthood" remarked George Bernard Shaw of his
associate Vedrenne, "it is not for nothing that he called his theatre *The
Queen's* . . . but why not The Alexandra?" In any event, on 8th
October, 1907, Vedrenne's *Queen's Theatre* opened on the corner of
Shaftesbury Avenue and Wardour Street. (Many of the new theatres
were built on corner plots, building restrictions now no longer
permitting the cramped conditions, with all the inherent fire and
health hazards which typified theatres of the previous centuries.)

The wind of change was undoubtedly blowing in all directions,
emphasised further when Vedrenne announced that evening dress
was to be optional in part of the dress circle. The style of the interior
was elegant and handsome, borrowing a little from Italian, Georgian
and Edwardian themes. Sadly, however, the foyer and rear of the
circles suffered bomb damage in the last war and it was not until the

late fifties that the theatre was reconstructed. Under the guidance of Hugh Casson, a new modern exterior was erected, while inside the original style was largely retained.

AUDITORIUM PLAN

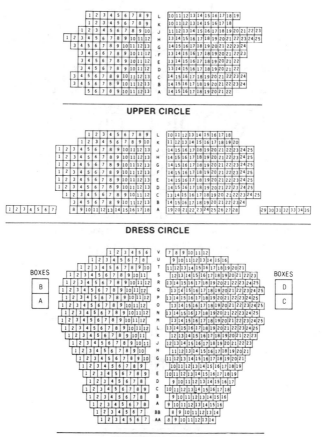

UPPER CIRCLE

DRESS CIRCLE

ORCHESTRA STALLS

THE
LEICESTER SQUARE TICKET BOOTH SELLS TICKETS FOR MANY WEST END PRODUCTIONS AT HALF PRICE.

*PLUS 75p SERVICE CHARGE

Open to personal callers only, on the day of performance from 12 noon for matinees and between 2.30pm and 6.30pm for evening performances. Tickets are sold for cash only, no credit cards or cheques are accepted

This is just one of the many activities organised by the Society of West End Theatre. For further information please turn to page 6.

At Last Going To The West End Theatre Is A Gift.

West End Theatre Gift Tokens.

Tokens are available in £1 and £5 units up to any amount and may be exchanged at most West End theatres (subject to availability), for the show of your choice.

For purchasing GIFT TOKENS by post, cheques including 30p for p + p, should be made payable to West End Theatre Managers Ltd. and sent to: Society of West End Theatre, Bedford Chambers, Covent Garden Piazza, London WC2E 8HQ or CALL TOKENLINE 01.379 3395 (24 hours) for purchase by credit card.

This is just one of the many activities organised by the Society of West End Theatre. For further information please turn to page 6.

THE LONDON THEATRE. ACT ON IT

Royal Court Theatre

Sloane Square, SW1W 3EE Map 5

Box Office; 10.00 to 20.00 hrs. **Tel:** Main House 730 1745 Theatre Upstairs 730 2554 **Bars:** 2 **Catering:** Snacks **Cloakroom:** Attendant **Seating:** 401 **Credit Cards:** Yes **Underground:** Sloane Square **Buses:** 11, 19, 22, 137.

The Royal Court could really be described as a 'theatregoer's theatre'. With a responsibility to foster new playwrights and theatrical talents of all kinds, it has become a nucleus of creativity – occasionally disturbing, sometimes shocking, constantly stimulating. And the effects are far reaching, for many of today's leading dramatists made their débuts at *The Royal Court* as have numerous successful West End productions.

The Royal Court has origins dating back to 1870 when a dissenting chapel was converted into a theatre known at first as *The New Chelsea*. Local residents apparently regarded the transformation without enthusiasm, remarking that there were already actors, boxes, a pit, money-taking at the doors, histrionics of all kinds and incredibly bad acting!

Royal Court

Destined for a short run, *The New Chelsea* became *The Belgravia* and before the end of 1870 had been converted into " . . . a bright little theatre capable of seating comfortably 1,100 persons. It is gorgeous in gilding, profuse in ornamentation and its hangings and box curtains are of a pinkish mauve satin . . . " Thus run the description in *"The Illustrated London News"* of 4th February, 1871. The name was then changed to *The Royal Court*.

Following the theatre's closure and subsequent demolition, manager John Clayton built a new theatre (the present building) on the east side of the square which opened in September, 1888. After suffering bomb damage in 1940, the theatre remained derelict until Robert Cromie renovated it for the London Theatre Guild in 1952. More improvements followed with the arrival of the English Stage Company in 1956 and in 1971 the old rehearsal rooms became *The Theatre Upstairs*.

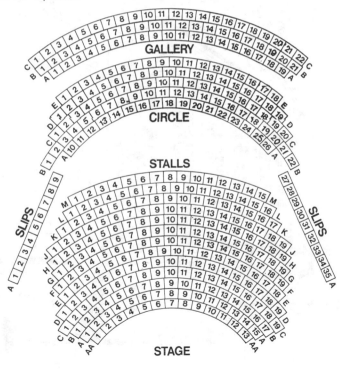

Royal Opera House

Covent Garden, WC2E 7QA **Map 2**

Box Office: 10.00 to 20.00 hrs. **Tel:** 240 1066 & 240 1911 **Bars:** 8 **Catering:** 4 Buffet Bars **Cloakroom:** Attendant **Seating:** 2,154 **Credit Cards:** Access, Visa, Diners Club, **Underground:** Covent Garden **Buses:** 1, 4, 6, 9, 11, 13, 15, 23, 68, 77, 170, 171, 172, 176, 188, 501, 502, 513.

Royal Opera House

For some people the name Covent Garden conjures up an image of the famous fruit and vegetable market, while for others it is *The Royal Opera House* — and, indeed, for 250 years they each went about their respective business side by side.

The first of the three theatres opened in 1732 and was one of the two London Theatres to hold a Patent permitting the performance of drama – the other being *The Theatre Royal*, Drury Lane. Apart from a few short seasons of Italian opera and an association with Handel, it was primarily devoted to drama – attracting to its stage such great names as David Garrick, Mrs. Siddons and the Kembles. However, on 19th September, 1808 it was burned down, taking with it Handel's organ and some manuscripts.

The new theatre, designed by Richard Smirke, was said to be the largest in Europe — Flaxman's bas-reliefs and statues, representing Comedy and Tragedy, have survived to this day and can now be seen behind the portico. Because of the vast cost of rebuilding, the new management attempted to raise the seat prices when the auditorium theatre opened in 1809, but this proved extremely unpopular and resulted in the famous 'Old Prices' Riots which lasted for 61 nights until the prices were reduced. In 1847 the theatre became *The Royal Italian Opera* but nine years later it too was destroyed by fire. Its replacement, which finally opened in 1858, was designed by Sir Edward Barry and remains today as sumptuous and magnificent as ever — with its great dome and fine Victorian auditorium, eminently regal in red, gold and cream. The chandelier has now been moved and many of the private boxes — which previously ran around all three tiers — have been opened up. However, the profile of the young Queen Victoria above the proscenium and the rows of cherubs which decorate the front of each tier (and reach a more advanced stage of womanhood at each descending level!) remain.

Some of the greatest names in the history of opera are associated with Covent Garden, including the legendary Patti, Nellie Melba, Caruso, Gobbi and Maria Callas. The late 19th and early 20th centuries saw the 'Golden Age' of the Opera House with extravagant Gala Performances – the Royal Box decked out in great glory and the programmes printed on white silk. This tradition was revived in 1977 with the Silver Jubilee Gala. Sir Thomas Beecham also played an important role in the theatre's development – although dedicated to opera, it was he who brought over Diaghilev's Russian Ballet and so started the ballet tradition. Since 1939 the theatre has been officially

Royal Opera House

known as *The Royal Opera House* and in 1946 it became the national home of both Opera and Ballet — the long list of the famous being joined by such celebrated names as Dame Ninette de Valois, Sir Frederick Ashton, Constant Lambert, Dame Margot Fonetyn,

Rudolph Nureyev and many others. The Sadler's Wells Ballet became The Royal Ballet in 1956 and in October 1968, The Covent Garden Opera became The Royal Opera.

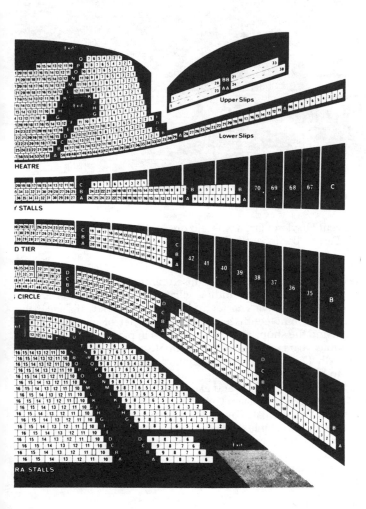

The Market, Covent Garden

OLD LONDON – COVENT GARDEN The Piazza from the South Side c 1720

The Covent Garden Piazza was laid out in 1631 by Inigo Jones for the Fourth Earl of Bedford; St. Paul's Church, at the western end, was built as the centre-piece of the Piazza development and was completed in 1638.

The open square became a recognised centre for the sale of fruit and vegetables from the surrounding villages, and in 1670 the Earl of Bedford obtained a royal charter from Charles II to hold a market in the Piazza. By the nineteenth century the character of the Market had changed, and the shops and booths erected in piecemeal fashion over the previous years were no longer adequate.

The sixth Duke of Bedford commissioned the architect Charles Fowler to design a new building, and the present Market was completed in 1830. The cast iron and glass roofs over the halls were erected in 1874-5 and 1889 by William Cubitt & Co., and are excellent examples of their kind which create covered public spaces unique in London.

The fruit and vegetable market moved out of Covent Garden in 1974 to new premises at Vauxhall, leaving behind a building much battered and altered, yet unquestionably worth keeping. Along with other market properties, it was purchased by the Greater London Council, and restoration work started in 1975.

The Market

Alterations to the basic structure and form have been kept to a minimum. The only major innovation has been the creation of two lower courtyards in the South Hall, otherwise the alterations are largely of internal layout and the provision of modern services. The public will find the Market an unusual and enjoyable shopping and eating experience. It represents a unique collection of shops and restaurants under literally two roofs, a useful addition to the London Theatre scene.

Forty-five trading units have now been formed within the building at basement, ground and first floor levels. These units, ranging in size from *large shops* on three levels to *tiny kiosks,* including shops, *a pub, two wine bars* and *various eating places.*

In addition some forty trading stands, salvaged from the Flower Market, have been re-erected for use by daily stallholders selling antiques on Mondays and crafts Tuesday to Saturday. Street entertainment may also be enjoyed at two pitches arranged by the GLC in front of St. Paul's Church and inside the building's North Hall. St. Paul's is now the Actors' church, with numerous memorials and tributes to the famous. The Bedford Chambers building, rebuilt to its original design in 1880 by the architect, Mr Cloutton, gives an idea of one of the side buildings to the Piazza.

At the south-eastern corner of the Piazza, is the former Flower Market now owned by the GLC. The ground floor has been leased to the London Transport Museum, with its collection of buses, trolley buses, trams, and trains, open everyday from 10.00 a.m. till 6.00 p.m. This is one of two museums housed in the former Flower Market. The National Theatre Museum, which will cover all aspects of the performing arts, is under construction.

OLD LONDON — COVENT GARDEN The Piazza from the West Side c 1840 (much the same today)

Royal Shakespeare Theatre

Stratford-upon-Avon, Warwickshire CV37 6BB

Box Office: 10.30 to 19.30 hrs. **Tel:** 295623 **Bars:** 3 **Catering:** Box Tree Restaurant and River Restaurant. Reservations tel: 293226 **Cloakroom:** Attendant **Seating:** 1,500 **Credit Cards:** Yes **Train:** InterCity fast train Euston to Coventry, change to bus or taxi, or Paddington to Stratford-upon-Avon, change at Leamington Spa **Bus:** Victoria Coach Station

The first home for Shakespeare's plays was, of course, the famous *Globe Theatre*, which was built on the south side of the Thames in 1599. It was burned down in 1613, rebuilt the year after and finally demolished in 1644. However, it was not until 1769 – during the jubilee celebrations of the great tragic actor David Garrick – that the idea of staging regular Shakespeare Festivals at his birthplace of Stratford, was seriously considered. Even then it took another century before a permanent Shakespeare Memorial was established.

The foundation stone was laid in 1877 and the theatre — designed by Dodgeshun and Unsworth — opened on Shakespeare's birthday, the 23rd April, 1879.

Royal Shakespeare Theatre

Soon achieving the status of a national theatre, *The Shakespeare Memorial* was granted a Royal Charter in 1925, but sadly, was destroyed by fire the following year, leaving only the museum and connecting bridge unscathed.

Thanks to the efforts of Sir Archibald Flower and to contributions from all over the world — especially from the USA — a new theatre was opened on 23rd April, 1932. In 1950/51 it was modernised and redecorated.

In 1982, the RSC undertook the most exciting new development of its history — the move to the Barbican Centre in the City of London, where, in the 1150 seat auditorium, the Company presents new plays and classics alongside its Shakespeare work.

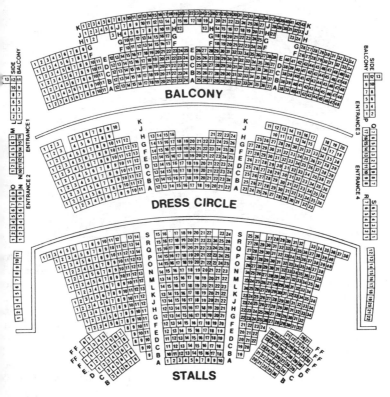

Sadler's Wells Theatre

Rosebery Avenue, EC1R 4TN   **Map 5**

Box Office: 10.30 am-7.30 pm Mon to Sat or until 6.30 pm when no
evening performance. **Tel:** 278 8916 **Bars:** 3 **Catering:** Snacks and
Buffet Restaurant **Cloakroom:** Attendant **Seating:** 1,500 **Credit Cards:**
Yes **Underground:** Angel **Buses:** From Central London: 19, 30, 38, 43,
73, 104, 214, 277, 279, 171 **Parking:** There is usually ample street
parking space in the vicinity of the theatre after 18.30.
Sadler's Wells stagecoach, a before and after to and from Main Line Rail
Stations.

Sadler's Wells had a varied career, going from great peaks of glory to
great depths of depression and disrepute. From 1916, it deteriorated
completely until nine years later, the amazing Lilian Baylis — who
had already brought drama, opera and ballet to *The Old Vic* — decided
to do the same for North London. Drama proved to be less popular in
North London however, and the theatre concentrated on ballet, under
the direction of Ninette de Valois, and opera. The Ballet Company was
so successful that it moved to Covent Garden and became The Royal
Ballet. The Opera Company was equally prosperous and moved to the
larger *London Coliseum* in August 1968, leaving *Sadler's Wells* free to

take on a new responsibility, namely to act as host to renowned Ballet, Mime and Opera companies form all over the world.

Sadler's Wells is the home of Sadler's Wells Royal Ballet which presents two seasons at the theatre each year; other companies appearing on a regular basis include London Contemporary Dance Theatre, Ballet Rambert and New Sadler's Wells Opera.

AUDITORIUM PLAN

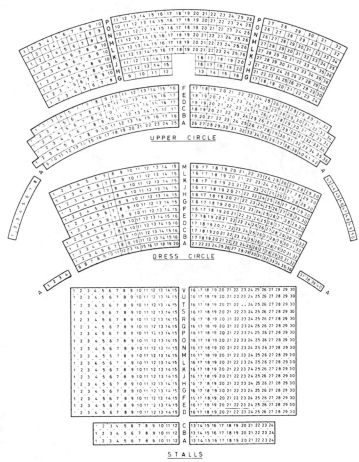

Savoy Theatre

Savoy Court, Strand, WC2R 0ET

Map 2

Box Office: 10.00 to 20.00 hrs. **Tel:** 836 8888 **Bars:** 4 **Catering:** Theatre/Dinner package — Simpsons in the Strand 6 to 7.30 p.m. **Cloakroom:** Attendant **Seating:** 1,122 **Credit Cards:** 379 6219 **Underground:** Covent Garden, Embankment **Buses:** 1, 6, 9, 11, 13, 15, 77, 170, 176.

Two of the many remarkable achievements of Richard D'Oyly Carte are connected with *The Savoy Theatre* – the establishment of a permanent 'home' for Gilbert and Sullivan's comic operas and the introduction of electric light to theatres.

D'Oyly Carte, W. S. Gilbert and Arthur Sullivan, while working together at *The Royalty Theatre* had already formed The Comedy Opera Company. When the lease on *The Royalty* expired, D'Oyly Carte decided not to renew it but instead to build his own theatre. Architect C. J. Phipps was commissioned for the design, and when *The Savoy* – situated on the Thames Embankment – opened, it was the first public building anywhere in the world to have electric light.

In 1929 a new two-tiered design, with interior decor by Basil Ionides, replaced the three-tiered auditorium. *"Country Life"* readers were told that, " . . . the general effect is one of glowing sunshine . . . the auditorium suffused with a golden light which the autumnal colours of the seats . . . warm into a glow . . . " The seats still reflect the glorious pinks and golds of autumn, although the overall decor has now been simplified. In the bar are some delightful prints depicting costumes used in various Gilbert and Sullivan operas.

AUDITORIUM PLAN

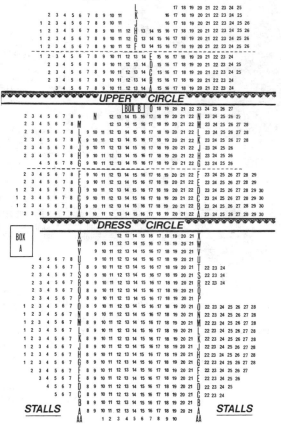

Shaftesbury Theatre

Shaftesbury Avenue, WC2H 8DP   **Map 2**

Box Office: 10.00 to 20.00 hrs. **Tel:** 379 5399 **Bars:** 5 **Catering:** Coffee
Cloakroom: Attendant **Seating:** 1358 **Credit Cards:** Yes
Underground: Tottenham Court Road, Holborn, Covent Garden
Buses: 1, 8, 14, 19, 22, 24, 25, 29, 38, 73, 176.

The musical "Hair" could be said, quite literally, to have brought the
house down' for, just as it was about to celebrate its 2,000th
performance at *The Shaftesbury Theatre* in July 1973, part of the ceiling
gave way and the theatre had to be closed! This event had rather
serious implications for, only a few months previously, *The
Shaftesbury* had been under threat of demolition when there were
plans to redevelop the site. However, with massive public support
and the efforts of the Save London's Theatres Campaign, it was
judged to be a " . . . building of special architectural or historic interest
. . . " The result was that the theatre was able to reopen in December
1974.

Shaftesbury

The original theatre was known as *The New Prince's* (the *New* was later dropped) and opened in 1911 to specialise in melodrama – with seats priced from sixpence to five shillings.

Today, *The Shaftesbury* is rich and ornate with its statuary, chandelier and French Renaissance style decorative work. The colour scheming is also exquisite, with elegant pink seats complementing perfectly the rose-coloured marbling and opulent gilding.

AUDITORIUM PLAN

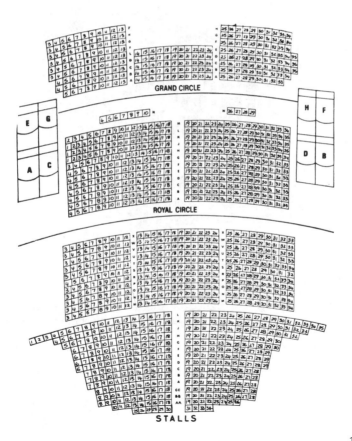

St Martin's Theatre

West Street, Cambridge Circus, WC2H 9NH   Map 2

Box Office: 10.00 to 20.00 hrs. **Tel:** 836 1443 **Bars:** 3 **Catering:** No **Cloakroom:** Attendant **Seating:** 550 **Credit Cards:** Yes **Underground:** Leicester Square **Buses:** 1, 14, 19, 22, 24, 29, 38.

The St. Martin's Theatre was planned to 'pair' with *The Ambassadors* close by, but while the latter was able to open in 1913, the outbreak of the First World War delayed the completion and opening of *The St. Martin's* until 23rd November, 1916.

Both theatres were designed by the sensitive hand of architect William Sprague, who was responsible for so many of the elegant little London theatres – including *The Albery, The Aldwych, The Strand* and *The Globe.* By now the great era of Victorian and Edwardian theatre-building was coming to its close – French influence had died away and a harder, more classical style known as 'neo-Georgian' was evolving.

The publication *"Architectural Review"* gave an account of the theatre at the time, remarking that " . . . its interior, instead of revelling in a lavish display of modelled plaster work, tricked out with

St Martin's

gold leaf and paint, has an intimate, almost domestic character . . . and gives one the impression of being a private theatre provided by some patron of the dramatic arts for the entertaining of his guests . . . " Apart from some damage to the facade during the blitz, the theatre remains virtually unchanged to this day, charming and cosy, with its red seating and dark wood panelling.

AUDITORIUM PLAN

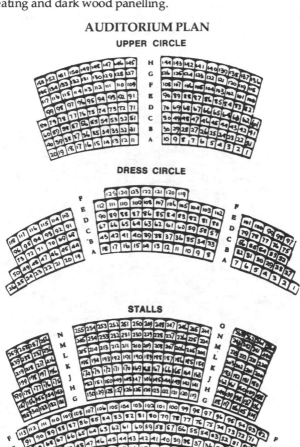

Strand Theatre

Aldwych, WC2B 5LD Map 2

Box Office: 10.00 to 20.30 hrs. **Tel:** 836 2660, 836 4143, 836 5190 **Bars: 4**
Catering: Yes **Cloakroom:** Attendant **Seating:** 925 **Credit Cards:** Yes
Underground: Covent Garden, Temple, Holborn **Buses:** 1, 6, 9, 11,
13, 15, 77, 170, 176, 188, 239, 305.

Stage door:
836 - 4144

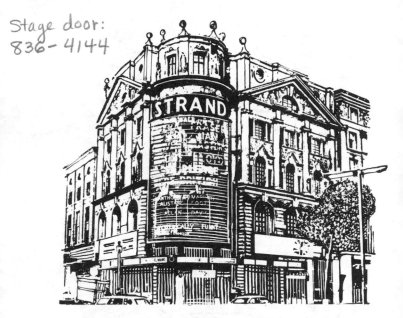

On 22nd May, 1905 *The Strand* (although it was known as *The Waldorf*
until 1909) became the first theatre to be built in the new Aldwych. It
was designed by William Sprague as one of a pair – the other being *The
Aldwych Theatre* – each occupying a similar corner site and separated
by the Waldorf Hotel. During this period, a great deal of construction
work was being carried out all over London and the Kingsway/
Aldwych development was to be a distinctive feature of the Imperial
capital.

Strand

The decor of *The Strand* was in the fashionable style of Louis XIV. *"The Era"* of 20th May, 1905 mentioned that " . . . One of the notable features is a magnificent circular ceiling in modelled plaster with finely gilt centrepiece and outer border and a boldly treated picture sweeping round the two . . . the bas relievo . . . which surmounts the proscenium represents Apollo in his chariot drawn by four spirited horses, attended by goddesses and cupids . . . "

The theatre has been redecorated a number of times – notably in 1930 – but overall has changed little since it was first built. Today, the auditorium is resplendent in turquoise, gold and cream with red seating. The Edwardian influence is also present in the foyer with its elegant statues and stairway, dominated by a large picture of London impresario, Henry Sherek.

AUDITORIUM PLAN

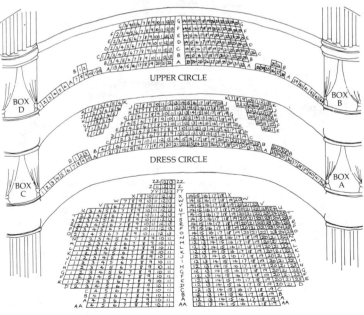

UPPER CIRCLE

DRESS CIRCLE

ORCHESTRA STALLS

The Old Vic

Waterloo Road, SE1 8NB

Map 5

Box Office: 10.00 to 20.00 hrs. **Tel:** 928 7616 Credit Card Booking: 261 1821 **Bars:** 3 **Catering:** Snacks Tel: 928 8197 for reservations **Cloakroom:** Attendant **Seating:** 1037 **Credit Cards:** Yes **Underground:** Waterloo **Buses:** 1, 1a, 4, 5, 68, 70, 76, 149, 171, 176, 188, 239, 501, 502, 507, 513.

If one person can be said to have contributed more to the development of the classical British theatre in modern times, then that person must be Lilian Baylis, who devoted almost forty years of her life to *The Old Vic*. In 1912, Lilian Baylis officially took over the theatre from her aunt, Emma Cons, a social reformer and herself something of a pioneer. In 1880, when she had come to *The New Victoria Palace* (as it was previously known), it was a bawdy, disreputable house. She refurbished it, changed the name to *The Royal Victoria Hall and Coffee Tavern* and turned it into " . . . a cheap and decent place of amusement on strict temperance lines . . . "

The 5th May, 1931 – when the first ballet was performed with Anton Dolin as the guest – marked the beginning of the Vic-Wells Ballet

120

The Old Vic

Company under the direction of Ninette de Valois. Lilian Baylis had already rebuilt *The Sadler's Wells Theatre* and eventually this was to specialise in opera and ballet while *The Old Vic* concentrated on drama.

The theatre suffered severe bomb damage in the war although the auditorium escaped, and even today has changed little since Victorian times. After closing for nine years it was renovated in 1950 and Sean Kenny later made further improvements to the stage before the arrival of the National Theatre Company in 1962 (the company moved to the South Bank in 1976).

From 1976 the theatre had various managements, including the touring company, Prospect Productions, until May 1981 when public subsidy was withdrawn altogether. The Old Vic was closed from that date until October 1983 when, after a £2.5 million facelift, it was reopened under the ownership of Canadian entrepreneur 'Honest' Ed Mirvish.

AUDITORIUM PLAN

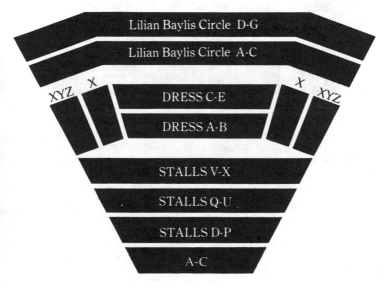

Vaudeville Theatre

Strand, WC2R ONH   **Map 2**

Box Office: 10.00 to 20.00 hrs. **Tel:** 836 9987 & 836 5645 **Bars:** 3
Catering: No **Cloakroom:** Attendant **Seating:** 694 **Credit Cards:** Yes
Underground: Charing Cross **Buses:** 1, 6, 9, 11, 13, 15, 77, 170, 176.

The Vaudeville, along with other theatres built around 1870, signified in
many ways the ending of an era. The theatre building boom which
followed brought with it many changes – foreign design influences,
higher safety standards and various technological improvements,
notably the introduction of electric light. Nevertheless, at the time,
The Vaudeville's own new system of lighting was something of an
innovation. A later historian wrote that " . . . Strode's sun-burners
radiated their brilliance from the centre of the ceiling; the footlights
contrary to the practice then obtaining, were entirely out of sight of
the audience . . . one advantage . . . was the removal of the unpleasant
vapour screen, which, in the old manner, was constantly rising
between the audience and the scene . . . "

Vaudeville

The outside of the theatre was left simply as numbers 403 and 404 Strand until 1891 when, as *"The Era"* of 10th January noted, ". . . These two houses have been pulled down and a handsome facade in Portland Stone erected . . ." This 'handsome facade' remains today — however, the inside was drastically altered in 1926. *The Vaudeville* was completely refurbished in 1969, and, with its elegant gold and cream decor, plum-coloured seats and glorious chandelier in the foyer — is undoubtedly one of London's most delightful little theatres, and is now owned by Michael Codron.

AUDITORIUM PLAN

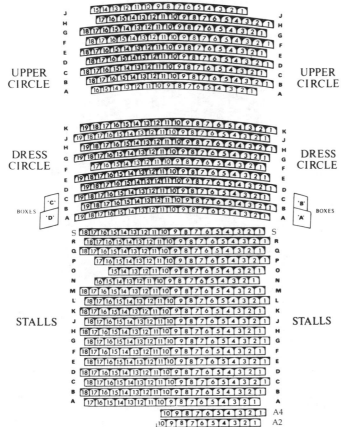

Victoria Palace Theatre

Victoria Street, SW1E 5EA

Map 5

Box Office: 10.00 to 20.00 hrs. **Tel:** 834 1317 **Bars:** 5 **Catering:** No **Cloakroom:** Attendant **Seating:** 1,565 **Credit Cards:** Yes **Underground:** Victoria **Buses:** 2, 10, 11, 16. 24, 25, 29, 36, 38, 39, 52, 149, 181, 185, 500, 503, 506, 507, 509.

The period 1880 until 1910 saw the music halls reach their peak in Britain. Hundreds of these lively establishments were built all over the country – to a far greater extent than were theatres or opera houses. Music halls were derived largely from the taverns, where food and drink automatically accompanied entertainment, and it was from just such origins *The Victoria Palace* evolved.

In 1910, Alfred Butt bought The Royal Standard Music Hall – previously The Royal Standard Tavern – which were the oldest premises in London to hold a licence for a music hall. Butt demolished the building, however, and commissioned Frank Matcham, the architect of numerous music halls all over the country, to design *The Victoria Palace*.

The classical facade once included a statue of the famous ballerina, Pavlova, who made her first London appearance at the theatre – but she was superstitious and refused to look up at it when she passed by! (It was taken down in the blitz and subsequently lost.) *"The Era"* of 4th November, 1911 described the interior as combining " . . . a maximum of comfort and convenience with a prevailing note of simplicity . . . The entrance hall through which the visitor passes to the stalls, dress circle and boxes has walls of grey marble with embellishments of gold mosaic and pillars of white Sicilian marble . . . "

Today, *The Victoria Palace* is a rich and atmospheric theatre, retaining much of its original style – the auditorium heavy and opulent and the foyer bright and elegant.

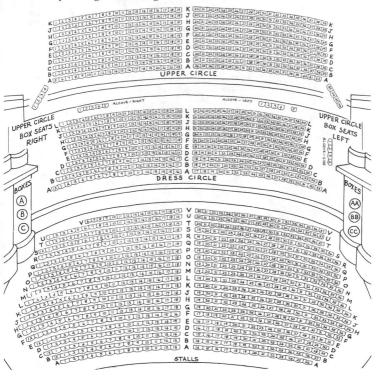

Westminster Theatre

Palace Street, Buckingham Palace Road,
SW1E 5JB.

Map 5

Box Office: 10.00 to 20.00 hrs. **Tel:** 834 0283 **Bar:** 1 **Catering:** Snacks and restaurant: Lunch 12.00 to 14.00 hrs; Dinner before performance 18.00 hrs. (reservations necessary) **Cloakroom:** Attendant **Seating:** 585 **Credit Cards:** Yes **Underground:** Victoria **Buses:** 2, 10, 11, 16, 24, 25, 29, 36, 38, 39, 52, 149, 181, 185, 500, 503, 506, 507, 509.

Credit card line: 834-0048

Stage door:
834-7882

Restaurant:
834-7781

In the early twenties the cinema age had dawned. A number of theatres had already been converted and many more new cinemas, including The St. James's Picture House, later *The Westminster Theatre*, were being built. The St. James's, which opened in 1923 was constructed on the site of an old chapel – the origins of which dated back to 1776 when the extrovert Reverend Dodd used the proceeds of his wife's lottery winnings and a legacy to pay for the building!

Eventually, after being a chapel-of-ease for St. Peter's, Eaton Square, it was sold in 1921.

In 1931, the building was taken over by Anmer Hall who transformed it into a theatre, adapting the crypt into dressing rooms and a green room and incorporating a circle into the auditorium. Today, *The Westminster* which Hall named after his old public school, is a delightful little theatre with its chandelier and tasteful auditorium decor of brown, green and white. There is a spacious restaurant and coffee/tea shop, open to theatregoers and non-patrons alike — and modern audio-visual facilities make the theatre a popular venue for business conventions and Induction Loop for Deaf patrons is now installed.

AUDITORIUM PLAN

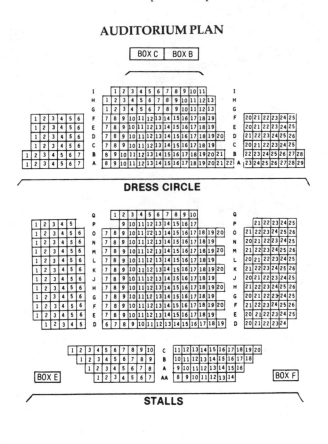

Wyndham's Theatre

Charing Cross Road, WC2H 0DA **Map 2**

Box Office: 10.00 to 20.00 hrs. **Tel:** 836 3028 Credit Card Booking: Tel. 379 6565 09.00-20.00 **Bars:** 2 **Catering:** No **Cloakroom:** Paralok **Seating:** 759 **Credit Cards:** Yes **Underground:** Leicester Square **Buses:** 1, 14, 19, 22, 24, 29, 38, 176.

When the Marquess of Salisbury was asked if he would permit a theatre to be built on his land between St. Martin's Lane and Charing Cross Road, he was not particularly enthusiastic – unless it be for Charles Wyndham, the actor manager, whose dramatic talents he greatly admired.

In fact, Wyndham, manager of *The Criterion Theatre* for some years, already had plans to build his own theatre, so the choice of site was an obvious one. The architect Sprague was commissioned to design the theatre on the same plot of land where he was later to be responsible for *The New Theatre* (now *The Albery*). Sprague's work was usually a blend of styles, but at the turn of the century he was particularly influenced by the wave of French fashion – and this is reflected in his theatre. *"The Era"* of 18th November, 1899 says " . . . The scheme of decoration is that of Louis XVI, and the colours used are turquoise blue and cream, relieved by judicious gilding . . . The ceiling of the auditorium contains paintings after Boucher, which are illuminated by a ring of concealed electric lights and a central sunlight covered by a crystal pendant . . . " Today, *Wyndham's* is one of the loveliest of London's small, intimate theatres. The colour scheme is still pale blue, cream and gold with dark blue seating. The bust over the proscenium is reputed to be that of actress Mary Moore – who eventually became Charles Wyndham's wife.

AUDITORIUM PLAN

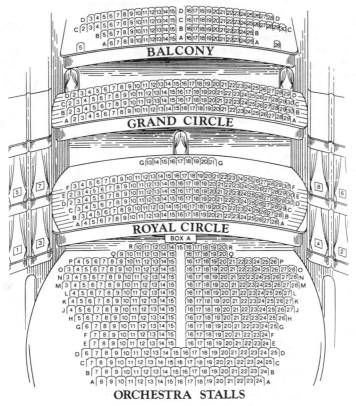

LONDON   FRINGE

'Fringe' or 'alternative theatre' are terms widely used to describe entertainment and performances that are not part of the traditional West End Theatre network. The movement began in the late 60's in small studios and converted experimental venues as a reaction to and to complement the standard fare offered by the well known theatre establishment.

Since then fringe theatre has assumed a life of its own and London offers a wealth of talent committed to presenting innovative works and new ways of looking at old favourites. Often working within tight budgets the emphasis is on the quality and intimacy of performance.

Details about fringe shows are to be found in the *Guardian* every Saturday on the Arts page, the Alternative Theatre column, but extensive coverage is given in magazines such as *'Time Out'* and *'City Limits'*. This information includes telephone numbers, times of performances, how to get there and a short synopsis of what to expect from the show.

The *British Alternative Theatre Directory* (published by John Offord Publications Ltd., 12 The Avenue, Eastbourne BN21 3YA) is a comprehensive guide to all the fringe has to offer.

Map by courtesy of *Theatre Despatch*, 853 0750.

THEATRE DESPATCH
P.O. BOX 633
LONDON SE7 7HE
01-853 0750

1   Africa Centre
2   Albany Empire
3   Almeida
4   Arts
5   Battersea Arts Centre
6   Bear Gardens
7   Bloomsbury
8   Bridge Lane
9   Bubble
10 Bush
11 Cafe
12 Phoenix
13 Chats Palace
14 Cockpit
15 Commonwealth Arts Centre
16 Cottesloe (NT)
17 Curtain
18 Croydon Warehouse
19 Drill Hall
20 Falcon
21 Factory
22 Finborough Arms
23 Gate at Notting Hill
24 Latchmere
25 Golden Lane
26 Canal Cafe
27 Half Moon
28 Hampstead
29 Hoxton Hall
30 Institute of Contemporary Arts
31 Jacksons Lane
32 Jeanetta Cochrane
33 Kings Head

34 Little Angel Marrionette
35 Lyric, Hammersmith
36 Man in the Moon
37 New End
38 Odyssey
39 Old Red Lion
40 Orange Tree, Richmond
41 Oval
42 Pindar of Wakefield
43 Pit (RSC)
44 Place
45 Polka
46 Posk
47 Riverside Studios
48 Soho Poly
49 Theatre Upstairs
50 Theatro Technis
51 Three Horseshoes
52 Tom Allen Centre
53 Tramshed
54 Tricycle
55 Theatre Royal, Stratford East
56 Upstream
57 Warehouse
59 Waterman's, Brentford
58 Young Vic
60 Sir Richard Steele

THEATRES

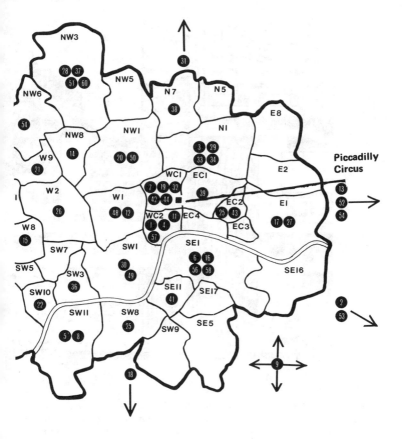

Concert halls

Concert lovers in London are undoubtedly privileged, for throughout the capital there are a variety of venues, which, between them cater for every kind of musical taste. And because each hall has its own very individual style – differing from the others in its architecture, decor and ambiance – every performance promises to be a completely unique experience. Take on the one hand *The Royal Albert Hall*, eminently Victorian and grandiose, majestically sited opposite the

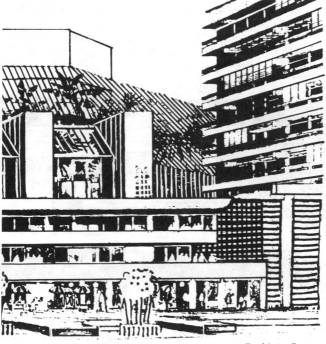

Barbican Centre

Albert Memorial, and compare it to the intimate and elegant *Wigmore Hall,* platform for many of this century's greatest performers. Then in the city, there is the Barbican Hall located in the Barbican Centre, one of the wonders of the modern world! Cross the river and there is yet another comparison to be made when one is confronted with the uncompromisingly modern *Royal Festival Hall* which makes up a part of the exciting South Bank Arts complex.

Barbican Hall

Silk Street, London EC2Y 8DS

Advance Booking: 638 8891/628 8795
For general information see 'Barbican Centre' — Page 36.

The Barbican Hall is home to the London Symphony Orchestra (London's only orchestra with a permanent base), who perform over 100 concerts throughout the year.

The auditorium, seating 2026 in three curved, raked tiers, provides excellent sightlines combined with a degree of intimacy not usually to

be found in a hall of this size. The interior decor of light-coloured pine contrasts attractively with the various dark tones of the extremely comfortable seating.

Outside the LSO season the hall functions as a concert hall for a wide range of performances from solo recitals to symphony orchestras, and includes a range of light entertainment — especially jazz. The Barbican Hall is also the Centre's main conference venue, and is equipped with simultaneous interpretation, amplification, broadcast and satellite relay, and projection facilities to meet the sophisticated requirements of today's conference organiser.

Royal Albert Hall

Kensington Gore, SW7 2AP   **Map 5**

Booking Office: 10.00 to 18.00 hrs. **Tel:** 589 8212 **Enquiries:** 589 3203
Bars: 10 **Catering:** Snacks **Cloakroom:** Attendant **Seating:** 5,000
approx. **Credit Cards:** 589 9465 **Underground:** Kensington High Street,
Knightsbridge, South Kensington **Buses:** Direct 9, 9A, 52, 73; To
Palace Gate 49; To Kensington Church Street 27, 28, 31; To South
Kensington 14, 30, 45, 74. Patrons wishing to travel east after 21.30
should travel to Hyde Park Corner and change.

Royal Albert Hall.

It had been the wish of Prince Albert, Queen Victoria's beloved
husband, to provide the nation with an Arts and Science Centre.
Although he died before his dream became reality the inscription high
up on the outside of *The Albert Hall* remembers " . . . This hall was
erected for the advancement of the Arts and Sciences and works of
industry of all nations in fulfilment of the intention of Albert, Prince
Consort . . . "

Royal Albert Hall

With the £180,000 profit resulting from the Great International Exhibition of 1851 (itself initiated by Prince Albert), an estate was purchased in South Kensington and various plans drawn up for the proposed Arts and Science Centre under the guidance of Prince Albert. On his death in 1861, work came to a halt but the scheme was again taken up by his son, the Prince of Wales in 1865, and construction duly started in 1867. The red brick and terra cotta building, which took four years to complete, is in the Italian Renaissance style, and some believe it is based on the Colosseum in Rome.

A number of eminent artists of the day were commissioned to depict 'the progress of the arts' for part of the exterior design – which extends 800 feet and is still a fine example of Victorian decorative art. The oval-shaped building was designed to accommodate 8,000 people under its lofty dome, in an auditorium consisting of a flat arena with three tiers of boxes, a balcony and a promenade gallery above. The hall was originally lit by 11,000 gas burners which could be ignited in ten seconds, but this system was superseded by electricity almost a century ago.

Queen Victoria opened *The Albert Hall* on 29th March, 1871 in the presence of the entire Royal Family and the Prime Minister, Mr Gladstone. Since then, it has had five reigning monarchs as its patron – and remains a monument to the Victorian Age which is completely unlike any other. It is awe-inspiring and it is magnificent. Step inside and one is immediately overwhelmed by the strong sense of patriotism and tradition which dominate its still intensely Victorian atmosphere.

The Albert Hall has been used for religious and political events, athletic contests, banquets, exhibitions and, most of all, for music. For over a century, many of the world's greatest celebrities have appeared here.

In July 1871, the first recital was played on the Great Organ — described at the time as being ". . . the greatest and most complete instrument in the world ..." In 1877 came the unforgettable Wagner concerts, conducted by the composer himself, with vocalists from the Beyreuth Festival. In 1886, there was the long series of Patti concerts which continued until her retirement. Since 1941, (following the bombing of the previous venue, *The Queen's Hall*), there has been the annual season of Henry Wood Promenade Concerts, Festivals, Sporting Occasions, Popular Concerts etc.

Royal Albert Hall

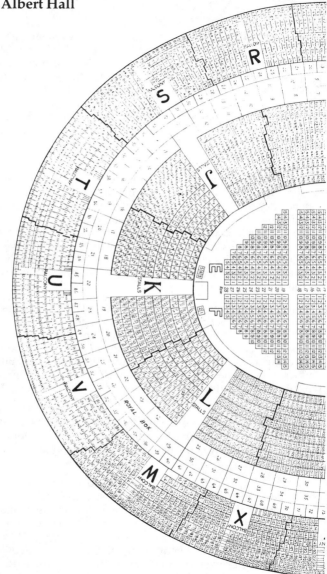

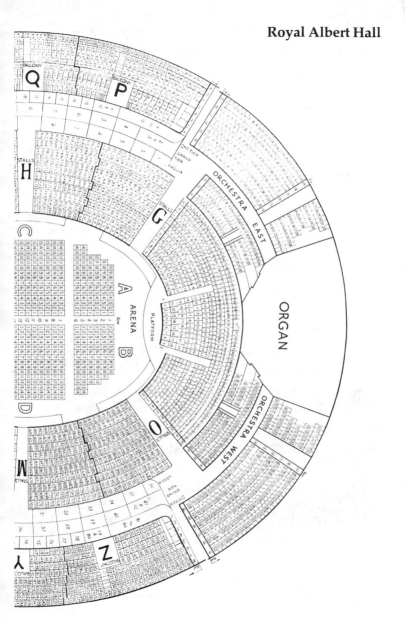

South Bank Concert Halls

Royal Festival Hall, Queen Elizabeth Hall and
Purcell Room

Map 5

Box Office: 10.00am-9.00pm weekdays, 1.30pm-9.00pm Sundays and Bank Holidays. **Tel:** 01-928 3191 10.00am-9.00pm weekdays. **Credit Cards:** (Access/Master Card and Barclaycard/Visa) in person or by telephone 01-928 8800. **Food and Drink:** Cafeteria service 10.00am-8.00pm (from 12 noon Sundays and Bank Holidays). Also licenced bars open normal hours, coffee bars in foyers. **Foyers Open:** from 10.00am — free lunchtime music, exhibitions and bookshop **Buses:** To Waterloo, Nos 1, 68, 70, 76, 171, 176, 177, 188, 507 **Underground:** Waterloo (Northern, Bakerloo) and Embankment (Northern, Bakerloo, District and Circle) **British Rail:** Waterloo **Car Parking:** NCP car parks nearby **Mailing List:** £3 per annum.

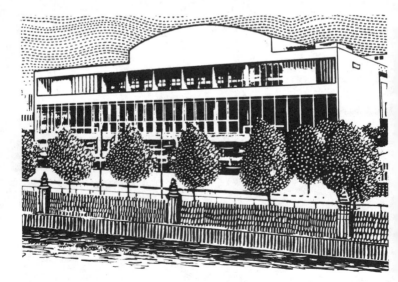

It is hard to imagine that, just after the war, the site which now houses London's handsome South Bank complex was little more than an area of dereliction. The concept of The South Bank Concert Halls was originally conceived in 1948 under Mr. Attlee's Government, when the London County Council (predecessors of the Greater London Council) offered to provide a permanent concert hall as their contribution to the Festival of Britain, planned for 1951.

The scheme was a far reaching one and the resulting Arts Centre now incorporates not only *The Royal Festival Hall, The Queen Elizabeth Hall* and *The Purcell Room* but also *The National Film Theatre and The Hayward Gallery* — all of which link up, via attractive walkways. *The Royal Festival Hall* building is spacious and impressive, with its broad stairways, lifts and large foyer, which allows audiences, invalids included, to assemble in ease and comfort. There are numerous bars, cafeterias, coffee bars and restaurants.

Royal Festival Hall/ Auditorium

Mr. Attlee laid the foundation stone of *The Festival Hall* in 1949, and two years later the ceremonial opening took place at an inaugural concert attended by King George VI and H.M. Queen Elizabeth. The Archbishop of Canterbury conducted a Service of Dedication and this was followed by a programme of British music.

Designed by Sir Robert Matthew and Sir Hubert Bennett, *The Festival Hall* has a large auditorium and can accommodate 2,909 people during the concert season. The hall is resplendent in elm panelling and red leather and boasts excellent acoustics, which in 1964, were given the added advantage of an 'assisted resonance system'. The platform can be raised or lowered to three different levels and a proscenium arch can be erected for ballet or other stage productions. Approximately 450 performances are given annually, of which about two-thirds are symphony concerts. The Festival Hall Organ, designed by Ralph Downes was installed in 1954 and inaugurated on 24th March of that year.

Royal Festival Hall (Auditorium)

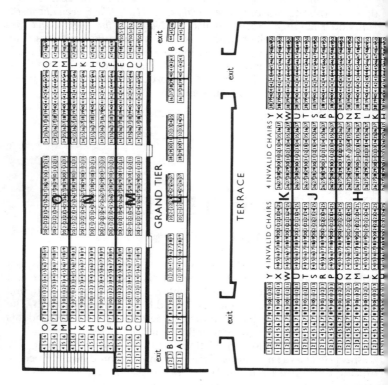

Royal Festival Hall

Royal Festival Hall/ Queen Elizabeth Hall

Some 750 events are staged annually in the two smaller auditoria and include small orchestral and chamber music recitals, poetry readings, conferences and film performances. *The Queen Elizabeth Hall* seats 1,100 people and has a modular platform comprising 13 independent sections, which can be raised or lowered to a wide range of tiered levels, plus projection facilities for 70mm, 35mm, and 16mm films. The inaugural concert on 1st March, 1967 was attended by Queen Elizabeth II and the opening concert included a programme of works by such composers as Purcell, Bliss, Arne and Britten.

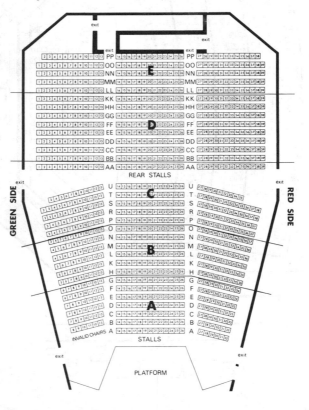

Royal Festival Hall/ Purcell Room

The Purcell Room, with a seating capacity of 372 is a small intimate hall, used for recitals by solo artistes and chamber groups. It is particularly suitable for the presentation of poetry and prose readings.

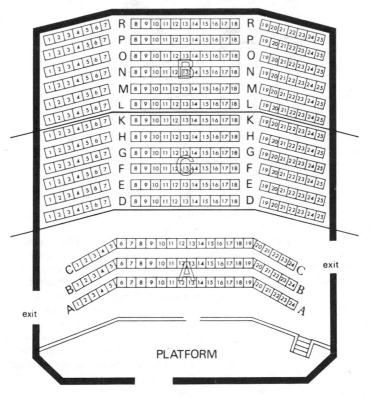

Wigmore Hall

Wigmore Street, W1H 9DF.

Map 1

Box Office: 10.00 to 20.00 hrs. **Tel:** 935 2141 **Bars:** 1 **Catering:** Snacks and coffee **Cloakroom:** Attendant **Seating:** 542 **Credit Cards:** Yes **Underground:** Bond Street **Buses:** 159.

The name Bechstein brings to most people's minds an image of magnificent grand pianos – but probably rather fewer people realise that Frederick Wilhelm Carl Bechstein was also the creator of what is now known as *The Wigmore Hall. The Bechstein Hall* opened in 1901 on a site next to Bechstein's showrooms in Wigmore Street. Designed in beautiful Renaissance style by Mr. Collcutt F.R.I.B.A. and built at a cost of almost £100,000 its near-perfect acoustics soon made it one of London's most popular venues for solo recitals and chamber music. Today's *Wigmore Hall*, still retaining its abundance of marble and alabaster, is as glorious as ever. When empty, one is struck by its innate elegance and dignity, yet when the hall is crowded with enthusiastic concert-goers, the atmosphere changes to one of great intimacy.

Wigmore Hall

The platform of *The Wigmore Hall* has welcomed most of this century's greatest performers including, since the twenties, a guitar recital by Segovia, numerous performances by Artur Rubinstein (who made his début here in 1912 when aged 25), and a never to be forgotten appearance of Prokofiev in 1931. Elisabeth Schwarzkopf made her London début at *The Wigmore Hall* in 1948, as did Daniel Barenboim in 1958 (aged 15 and wearing short trousers!) From the fifties works by Benjamin Britten were heard, sung by Peter Pears to the composer's accompaniment. *The Wigmore Hall's* 75th Anniversary celebrations in 1976 included special recitals by Artur Rubinstein, Elisabeth Schwarzkopf, Julian Bream and Peter Pears.

AUDITORIUM PLAN

PLAN OF GROUND FLOOR

PLAN OF BALCONY

Where to Eat

The theatre itself creates a marvellous sense of occasion and somehow a pleasant drink or two with a meal before or after the performance all goes towards increasing the enjoyment. But where's the best place to go? Can you get a drink at the theatre? Does anywhere serve a good meal at 6pm? Or where do you go if you feel like dining after the show?

'The London Theatre Scene' has the answers for you — whether you're looking for 'fast food' 'pub-grub' or say, French cuisine. All you have to do is look up the Street Map relevant to your theatre and you'll find alongside a wide selection of recommendations offering whichever standards of cuisine, comfort, price, decor and ambience you require. All have been personally visited and are especially recommended.

Note that Wine Bars tend to offer 'bistro-type' fare in more comfortable surroundings than pubs, though both have their own 'special' atmosphere. Hot and cold snacks and salads are generally available at both.

Pub hours: 11.00-15.00, 17.30-23.00
Sun: 12.00-14.00, 19.00-22.30

Restaurant hours: 17.00-23.30*, this is usually last order time and not the closing time.

Pre-theatre set meals are available at some restaurants at very reasonable prices, check when making reservations.

Symbols: £ = about £5.00, ££ = about £10.00, £££ = about, £15.00, £££* = over £15.00 (wine is not included)
● = Open after theatre

Credit Cards: A - Access, AX - American Express, B - Barclay (Visa), DC - Diner's Card

Where to Eat

Where to Eat — Piccadilly - Soho - St. Martins Lane

A L'ECU DE FRANCE
*French £££** ● **Map p 149**
12.30-15.00, 18.30-23.00
Closed Sat L. Sun (must book)
Credit Cards: A, AX, B, DC.
110 Jermyn St. **Tel: 930 2837**

AU JARDIN DES GOURMETS
*French £££** ● **Map p 149**
Closed Sat L. Sun (must book)
Credit Cards: A, AX, B, DC.
5 Greek St. **Tel: 437 1816**

BENTLYS
Seafood £££ ● **Map p 149**
12.00-14.45, 18.00-22.30
Closed Sun (must book)
Credit Cards: most
11-15 Swallow St. **Tel: 734 4756**

BEOTY'S
Greek £££ ● **Map p 149**
12.15-15.00, 17.30-23.30
Closed Sun
Credit Cards: A, AX, B, DC.
79 St. Martin's Lane **Tel: 836 8768**

BIANCHIS
Italian ££ ● **Map p 149**
12.00-14.45, 18.00-23.15
Closed Sun (must book)
Credit Cards: A, AX, B, DC.
21a Frith St. **Tel: 437 5194**

BRAGANZA
Seafood £££ ● **Map p 149**
12.30-14.30, 18.15-23.15
Closed Sun (must book)
Credit Cards: A, AX, B, DC.
57 Frith St. **Tel: 437 5412**

CAFE ROYAL GRILL
*Grills £££** ● **Map p 149**
12.00-15.00, 18.00-23.00
Closed No (must book)
Credit Cards: A, AX, B, DC.
68 Regent St. **Tel: 439 6320**

CHEZ SOLANGE
French £££ ● **Map p 149**
12.15-15.15, 17.30-00.15
Closed Sun (must book)
Credit Cards: A, AX, B, DC.
35 Cranbourne St. **Tel: 836 0542**

CHEZ VICTOR
French ££ ● **Map p 149**
12.00-14.30, 18.00-23.15
Closed Sun (must book)
Credit Cards: AX
45 Wardour St. **Tel: 437 6523**

CHUEN-CHENG-KU
Chinese £ ● **Map p 149**
11.00-23.30
Closed No
Credit Cards: Yes
17 Wardour St. **Tel: 437 3509**

CORK & BOTTLE (Wine Bar)
Buffet £ ● **Map p 149**
11.00-14.45, 17.30-22.45
Open Sun: 12.00-14.30, 17.00-22.30
Credit Cards: A, AX, B, DC.
44 Cranbourne St. **Tel: 734 7807**

DU ROLLO
French ££ ● **Map p 149**
12.30-15.00, 17.45-23.15
Closed Sun (must book)
Credit Cards: A, AX, B, DC.
20 Greek St. **Tel: 734 6991**

FINO'S (Wine Bar)
Buffet £ ● **Map p 149**
11.30-15.00, 17.30-23.30
Closed Sundays
Credit Cards: A
19 Swallow St. **Tel: 734 2049**

FINO'S (Wine Bar and Restaurant)
Buffet £ ● Map p 149
11.30-15.00, 17.30-23.30
Closed Sun
Credit Cards: A, AX, B, DC.
104 Charring Cross Rd **Tel: 836 1077**

GAY HUSSAR
Hungarian £££ ● Map p 149
12.30-14.30, 17.30-23.30
Closed Sun
Credit Cards: No
2 Greek St. **Tel: 437 0973**

INIGO JONES
French £££* ● Map p 149
12.30-14.30, 17.30-23.30
Closed Sat L. Sun (must book)
Credit Cards: A, AX, B, DC.
14 Garrick St. **Tel: 836 6456**

IVY
French £££* ● Map p 149
12.15-14.30, 18.15-23.15
Closed Sat L. Sun (must book)
Credit Cards: A, AX, B, DC.
1-5 West St. **Tel: 836 4751**

KETTNERS
Haute Cuisine (Popular) Map p 149
£ ●
11.00-24.00
Closed No
Credit Cards: A, AX, B, DC.
29 Romilly St. **Tel: 734 6112**

LA BUSSOLA
Italian £££ ● Map p 149
12.00-15.00, 18.00-24.00
Closed Sat L. Sun
Credit Cards: A, AX, B, DC.
42 St. Martin's Lane **Tel: 240 1148**

LA CAPANNINA
Italian ££ ● Map p 149
12.00-15.00, 18.00-23.30
Closed Sat L. Sun (must book)
Credit Cards: A, AX, B, DC.
24 Romilly St. **Tel: 437 2473**

L'EPICURE
French (Flambe's) £££ ● Map p 149
12.00-14.30, 18.00-23.15
Closed Sat L. Sun (must book)
Credit Cards: A, AX, B, DC.
28 Frith St. **Tel: 437 2829**

L'ESCARGOT
French £££ ● Map p 149
12.15-14.30, 18.30-23.15
Closed Sat L. Sun (must book)
Credit Cards: A, AX, B, DC.
48 Greek St. **Tel: 437 2679**

MANZI
Seafood £££ ● Map p 149
12.00-14.40, 17.30-23.30
Closed Sun L. (must book)
Credit Cards: A, AX, B, DC.
1 Leicester St. **Tel: 734 0224**

MARIO & FRANCO TERRAZZA
Italian £££ ● Map p 149
12.00-15.30, 18.00-23.30
Closed No (must book)
Credit Cards: AX, B, A, DC.
19 Romilly St. **Tel: 734 2504**

MARTINEZ
Spanish £££ ● Map p 149
12.00-15.00, 17.15-23.30
Closed No
Credit Cards: A, AX, B, DC.
25 Swallow St. **Tel: 734 5066**

MAXIM'S
French £££* ● Map p 149
12.30-15.00, 18.30-23.45
Closed Sun (must book)
Credit Cards: A, AX, B, BC.
Panton St. **Tel: 839 4809**

PAPPAGALLI'S
Pizza £ ● Map p 149
12.00-24.00
Closed Sun
Credit Cards: A. B.
7/9 Swallow St. **Tel: 734 5182**

Where to Eat — Piccadilly - Soho - St. Martins Lane

Trocadero

PIZZA EXPRESS
Pizza £ ●   Map p 149
11.30-24.00
Closed No
Credit Cards:
10 Dean St.   Tel: 437 9595

POON'S & CO.
Chinese ££ ●   Map p 149
12.00-23.30
Closed Sun
Credit Cards: No
4 Leicester St.   Tel: 437 1528

RUGANTINO
Italian £££ ●   Map p 149
12.00-14.30, 18.00-23.30
Closed Sun
Credit Cards: A, AX, B, DC.
26 Romilly St.   Tel: 437 5302

SHEEKEY'S
English-Seafood £££ ●   Map p 149
12.30-15.00, 17.30-23.30
Closed Sun (must book)
Credit Cards: A, AX, B, DC.
28 St Martin's Ct.   Tel: 240 2565

SURPRISE
American ££ ●   Map p 149
12.00-15.00, 17.30-23.15
Closed only Sunday Branch
11.45-15.00
Credit Cards: A, AX, B, DC.
12 Gt. Marlborough St. Tel: 434 2666

SWISS CENTRE (4 Restaurants)
Swiss, Gr. Fr. ££ ●   Map p 149
12.00-24.00
Closed No
Credit Cards: A, AX, B, DC.
Leicester Square   Tel: 734 1291

TOURMENT D'AMOUR
French £££ ●   Map p 149
12.00-14.00, 18.30-23.30
Closed Sat L. Sun (must book)
Credit Cards: A, AX, B, DC.
19 New Row, (C. Gdn.) Tel: 240 5348

BROOKES PIE HOUSE
English ££ ●   1
12.00-24.00
Open 7 days a week
Credit Cards: A, AX, B, DC.
Rupert Street Junction at The Trocadero, 7 Rupert Street, London W1
Tel: 439 8476

CAFE MONTMARTRE
French £££ ●   1
12.15-15.00, 18.15-24.00
Open 7 days a week
Credit Cards: A, AX, B, DC.
The Trocadero, Coventry Street, London W1   Tel: 439 8476

There are two wine bars in the International Village — Tino's in the Italian Piazza and the French wine bar in the French Quarter. Also in the French Quarter — the croissanterie and crêperie and in the Italian Piazza — the pizza/pasta section and the ice cream parlour.

VILLA VENEZIA (Mario & Franco)
Italian ££ ●   1
12.15-15.00, 18.15-24.00
Open 7 days a week
Credit Cards: A, AX, B, DC.
The Trocadero, Coventry Street, London W1   Tel: 439 8476

VEERASWAMY'S
Indian ££ ●   Map p 149
12.00-14.45, 17.30-23.30
Closed No
Credit Cards: A, AX, B, DC.
101 Regent St.   Tel: 734 1401

WHEELER'S
Seafood ££4 ●   Map p 149
12.30-14.30, 18.00-22.45
Closed Sun (must book)
Credit Cards: A, AX, B, DC.
19 Old Compton St.   Tel: 437 2708

Where To Eat—Strand - Covent Garden

THEATRES:

1	D7	*Adelphi*
3	C8	*Aldwych*
12	C7	*Drury Lane*
14	D7	*Duchess*
16	C7	*Fortune*
20	C7	*New London*
26	C8	*Royality*
27	C7	*Royal Opera*
29	D7	*Savoy*
31	D8	*Strand*
32	D7	*Vaudeville*

WHERE TO EAT:

89	C7	Ajimura
90	D7	Bates
91	C7	Bertorelli
92	D7	Blakes
93	D7	Boulestin
94	C7	Brahms & Liszt
96	D7	Flounders
127	C7	Frere Jacques
126	C7	Giardino's
97	C7	Interlude de Tabaillau
98	D7	Joe Allens
99	C7	Le Cafe des Amis dù Vin
100	D7	Le Cafe du Jardim
101	D7	La Scala
102	C7	L'Opera
103	D7	Luigis
104	C7	Magno's
105	C7	Marquis of Anglesey
106	C7	Maxwells
107	D7	McDonald's
108	C7	Nag's Head
109	C6	Neal Street
110	D7	Penny's
111	D6	Plummers
112	D7	Poons
113	D7	Porters
114	D7	Punch & Judy
115	D7	Rules
116	D7	Savoy Hotel Grill
117	C7	Simoni
118	D7	Simpsons in the Strand
119	D7	Strand Palace Hotel
120	D7	The Grange
121	D7	Thomas de Quincy
122	D7	Tuttons
123	C8	Waldorf Hotel
125	D7	Voltair's

HOTELS:

39	C7	Drury Lane
40	C8	Howard
41	D5	Pastoria
42	D5	Piccadilly
43	D5	Royal Angus
44	D7	Savoy
46	D7	Strand
47	C8	Waldorf

153

AJIMURA
Japanese ££ ● **Map p 153**
12.00-14.30, 18.00-23.00
Closed Sat L. Sun (must book)
Credit Cards: A, AX, B, DC.
51-53 Shelton St. **Tel: 240 0178**

BATES
English ££ ● **Map p 153**
12.00-15.00, 17.30-23.30
Closed No
Credit Cards: A, AX, B, DC.
11 Henrietta St. **Tel: 240 7600**

BERTORELLI'S
Italian ££ ● **Map p 153**
12.00-15.00, 18.00-23.30
Closed Sun (must book)
Credit Cards: A, AX, B, DC.
44 Floral St. **Tel: 836 3969**

BERTORELLI'S (Wine Bar)
Buffet £ ● **Map p 153**
Pub hours
Closed No
Credit Cards:
44 Floral St. **Tel: 836 1868**

BLAKES (Wine Bar)
Buffet £ ● **Map p 153**
11.30-23.00
Closed No
Credit Cards: A, B.
34 Wellington St. **Tel: 836 5298**

BOULESTIN
French £££* ● **Map p 153**
12.30-14.30, 19.30-23.15
Closed Sat L. Sun (must book)
Credit Cards: A, AX, B, DC.
1A Henrietta St. **Tel: 836 7061**

BRAHMS & LIST (Wine Bar)
Buffet £ ● **Map p 153**
11.30-15.00, 17.30-23.45
Closed Sat and L. Sun
Credit Cards: AX, B, A, DC.
19 Russell St. **Tel: 240 3661**

FLOUNDERS
Sea Food ££ ● **Map p 153**
12.30-14.30, 17.30-23.30
Closed Sun (must book)
Credit Cards: A, AX, B, DC.
19 Tavistock St. **Tel: 836 3925**

FOOD FOR THOUGHT
Buffet £ **Map p 153**
12.00-20.00
Closed Sat, Sun
Credit Cards: No.
31 Neal Street **Tel: 836 0239**

FRERE JACQUES
Seafood £££ ●
12.00-15.00, 18.00-23.30
Closed Sunday 14.30
Credit Cards: All Cards
38 Long Acre, C. Gdn. **Tel: 836 7823**

GIARDINO'S
Italian £££ ● **Map p 153**
12.00-15.00, 18.00-01.00
Closed. No
Credit Cards: All Cards
32 Long Acre, C. Gdn. **Tel: 836 8529**

INTERLUDE DE TABAILLAU
French £££ ● **Map p 153**
12.00-14.00, 19.00-23.30
Closed Sat L. Sun (must book)
Credit Cards: A, AX, B, DC.
7 Bow St. **Tel: 379 6473**

JOE ALLENS
American ££ ● **Map p 153**
12.00-01.00
Sunday 12.00-24.00 Closed Christmas
Credit Cards: No
13 Exeter St. **Tel: 836 0651**

LA SCALA
Italian ££ ● **Map p 153**
12.00-15.00, 17.30-23.30
Closed Sat L. Sun
Credit Cards: A, AX, B, DC.
35 Southampton St. **Tel: 240 1030**

LE CAFE DES AMIS DU VIN
French ££ ●   **Map p 153**
11.30-24.00
Closed Sun.
Credit Cards: A, AX, B, DC.
11 Hanover Pl.   **Tel: 379 3444**

LE CAFE DU JARDIN
French £££ ●   **Map p 153**
12.00-14.30, 18.00-23.30
Closed Sun and Sat Lunch
Credit Cards: A, AX, B, DC.
28 Wellington St.   **Tel: 836 8769**

L'OPERA
French £££ ●   **Map p 153**
12.15-15.00, 18.00-24.00
Closed Sat L. Sun (must book)
Credit Cards: A, AX, B, DC.
32 Queen St.   **Tel: 405 9020**

LUIGI'S
Italian £££ ●   **Map p 153**
12.15-15.00, 18.00-23.30
Closed Sun (must book)
Credit Cards: A, B.
15 Tavistock St.   **Tel: 240 1795**

MAGNO'S BRASSERIE
French ££ ●   **Map p 153**
12.00-14.30, 18.00-23.30
Closed Sat L. Sun
Credit Cards: A, AX, B, DC.
65a Long Acre   **Tel: 836 6077**

MARQUIS OF ANGLESEY (Pub)
Buffet £ ●   **Map p 153**
Pub Hours
Closed No
Credit Cards: No
39 Bow St.   **Tel: 240 3216**

MAXWELLS
American £ ●   **Map p 153**
12.00-24.00
Closed No
Credit Cards: B, A.
16/17 Russell St.   **Tel: 836 0303**

McDONALDS
American £ ●   **Map p 153**
06.00-23.00
Closed No
Credit Cards: No
35 Strand

NAGS HEAD
Buffet £ ●   **Map p 153**
Pub Hours
Closed No
Credit Cards: No
10 James St.   **Tel: 836 4678**

NEAL STREET
International £££ ●   **Map p 153**
12.30-15.00, 19.15-23.00
Closed Sat, Sun (must book)
Credit Cards: A, AX, B, DC.
26 Neal St.   **Tel: 836 8368**

PENNY'S (Wine Bar)
Buffet £ ●   **Map p 153**
11.30-15.00, 17.30-23.00
Closed Sat L. Sun
Credit Cards: A, B, AX.
6 King St.   **Tel: 836 4553**

PLUMMERS
American-English ££ ● **Map p 153**
12.00-14.30, 18.00-23.30
Closed Sat L. Sun (must book)
Credit Cards: A, AX, B, DC.
33 King St.   **Tel: 240 2534**

POONS OF COVENT GARDEN
Chinese £££ ●   **Map p 153**
Closed Sun. Advisable to book.
Credit Cards: AX, B, DC.
41 King Street
     Tel: 240 1743

PORTERS
English £ ●   **Map p 153**
12.00-15.00, 17.30-23.30
Closed No
Credit Cards: A, B.
17 Henrietta St.   **Tel: 836 6466**

Where To Eat—Strand - Covent Garden

PUNCH & JUDY (Pub)
Buffet £ ● **Map p 153**
Pub Hours
Closed No
Credit Cards: No
40 The Market, C.Gdn. **Tel: 836 1750**

RULES
English £££ ● **Map p 153**
12.15-14.30, 18.00-23.15
Closed Sat L. Sun (must book)
Credit Cards: A, AX, DC, Visa.
35 Maiden Lane **Tel: 836 5314**

SAVOY HOTEL GRILL
International £££* ● **Map p 153**
12.30-14.30, 18.00-23.15
Closed Sat L. Sun
Credit Cards: A, AX, B, DC.
Strand & Embankment **Tel: 836 4343**
River Restaurant £££* ●
12.30-17.30, 19.20-23.30
(Dancing from 20.30
Sun 19.00-22.00)

SIMONI
Italian £££ ● **Map p 153**
12.00-14.30, 18.00-23.30
Closed Sat L. Sun
Credit Cards: A, AX, B, DC.
43 Drury Lane **Tel: 836 8296**

SIMPSON'S IN THE STRAND
English £££ ● **Map p 153**
12.00-15.00, 18.00-22.00
Closed Sun (must book)
Credit Cards: A, B.
100 Strand **Tel: 836 9112**

STRAND PALACE HOTEL
Coffee Shop £ **Map p 153**
7.00-00.30
Italian Connection £££
Closed Sun
Credit Cards: A, AX, B, DC.
Mash Bar Pub hours
L'Osteria Bar 17.30-19.30
Carvery Rest. 12.00-14.30,
17.30-22.00 **Tel: 836 8080**

SHERLOCK HOLMES (Pub)
Buffet £ ● **Map p 13**
Pub Hours
Closed No
Credit Cards: No
10 Northumberland St. **Tel: 930 2644**

THE GRANGE
Franco-British £££ ● **Map p 153**
12.30-14.30, 19.30-23.30
Closed Sat L. Sun
Credit Cards: AX
39 King St. **Tel: 240 2939**

THOMAS DE QUINCY
French £££ ● **Map p 153**
12.00-14.30, 18.00-23.15
Closed Sun and Sat Lunch
(must book)
Credit Cards: A, AX, B, DC.
36 Tavistock St. **Tel: 240 3972**

TUTTONS
Franco-British ££ ●
12.00-23.30
Closed No
Credit Cards: A, AX, B, DC.
11 Russell St. **Tel: 836 1167**

VOLTAIR'S (Wine Bar)
Buffet £ ● **Map p 153**
11.00-15.00, 17.30-23.00
Closed Sun
Credit Cards: Most
41 Maiden Lane **Tel: 240 2843**

WALDORF HOTEL
Palm Court ££ **Map p 153**
English
10.00-02.00 (buffet lunch)
Sun 10.30-12.00
Tea 15.30-18.00
Credit Cards: A, AX, B, DC.
Footlights Bar Pub hours
Closed Sat & Sun
Aldwych **Tel: 836 2400**

No question about it.

It's got to be...

Time Out

London's Best-Selling Guide for Theatre

Where To Eat — South Bank

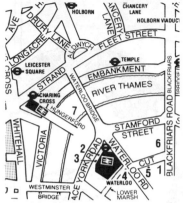

Royal Festival Hall

CAFETERIA
Buffet £
10.00-18.00 Fri, Sat and
Sun 10.00-20.00
Credit Cards: No

FOYERS
Buffet £
10.00-20.00, Sun 12.00-20.00
Credit Cards: A, AX, B, DC.
Tel: 928 3246

National Theatre

RESTAURANT
Dinner - 17.30-23.00. Closed Sun. Sat
Buffet L. 15.15-14.30

LYTTELTON THEATRE
Long Bar - Pub hours. Closed Sun.
Box Office Buffet 10.00-23.00 Closed
Sun. *Circle Bar* - Perf. days only,
17.30 to end of interval. *Buffet* - 12.00-
20.00. Closed Sun.

OLIVIER THEATRE
*Bars and buffets open performance days
only.*
Two Stalls Bars - 18.00 to end of last
interval. *Two Mezzanine Buffets* -
From 1½ hours before performance.
Circle Bar - 18.00 to end of interval.
Circle Coffee Bar - Interval only.

COTTESLOE THEATRE
Open from 1½ hours before performance until int. *Bars & Buffet.*

ACROPOLIS
Greek ££ (for parties) ●   1
8.30-21.00
Closed Sun
Credit Cards: No
43 The Cut   **Tel: 928 3689**

CAFE DE LA GARE
French ££ ●   2
12.00-14.30, 18.00-22.00
Closed Sat, Sun (must book)
Credit Cards: All.
19 York Road   **Tel: 928 9761**

IL PAPAGALLO
Italian ££ ●   3
12.00-23.00
Closed Sun
Credit Cards: Most.
35 York Road   **Tel: 928 1003**

LA BARCA
Italian ££ ●   4
12.00-14.30, 19.00-23.30
Closed Sat L. Sun (must book)
Credit Cards: A, AX, B, DC.
81 Lower Marsh   **Tel: 261 9221**

PHILLIPPE'S (Wine Bar)
Buffet £ ●   5
Pub hours
Closed Sat. Sun
Credit Cards: No
53 The Cut   **Tel: 633 9487**

SOUTH OF THE BORDER
International ££ ●   6
12.00-14.30, 18.00-23.30
Closed Sat L. Sun
Credit Cards: A, AX, B, DC.
8 Joan Street   **Tel: 928 6374**

THE ARCHDUKE (Wine Bar)
Buffet ££ ● (Restaurant)   7
11.00-15.00, 17.30-23.00
Closed Sat L. Sun
Credit Cards: A, AX, B, DC.
Belvedere Road   **Tel: 928 9370**

Mermaid Theatre

RIVERSIDE RESTAURANT
English ££ ●
12.00-14.30, 18.00-23.30
Closed Sun (must book)
Credit Cards: A, B.   **Tel: 236 0496**

BUFFET BAR
Buffet £
12.00-14.30, 17.00-21.30
Closed Sun
Credit Cards: No

BRIDGE & DOCK YARD BARS
Pub hours

Barbican Centre

THE CUT ABOVE
English ££
12.00-15.00, 18.00-½ hour
after the end of last performance.
Reservations advisable.
Credit Cards: A, AX, B, DC.
Level 7   **Tel: 588 3008**

THE WATERSIDE CAFE
Buffet £ ●
10.00-20.00, Sun 12.00-20.00
Credit Cards: A, AX, B, DC.
Level 5   **Tel: 638 4141 Ext 351**

WINE ON SIX (Wine Bar)
5.30-9.00pm Mon-Sat.
Credit Cards No.
Level 6
*There are bars, coffee and snack bars in
the Foyers — Barbican Hall and
Barbican Theatre, Levels 3, 5, 6. Some
keep pub hours, others open for
performances only.*

CHISWELL ST. VAULTS (Wine Bar)
Buffet £   3
Pub hours
Closed Sat. Sun
Credit Cards: AX, DC, A, B.
Chiswell St.   **Tel: 588 5733**

CORNEY & BARROW (also Wine
Bar)
British-French ££   4
11.30-15.00, 17.00-20.30
Closed Sat & Sun (must book)
Credit Cards: A, AX, B, DC.
118 Moorgate   **Tel: 628 2898**

RAVELLO
Italian ££ ●   6
12.00-15.00, 18.00-23.30
Closed Sun (must book)
Credit Cards: A, AX, B, DC.
42 Old St.   **Tel: 253 6279**

THE KING'S HEAD (Pub)
Buffet £ ●   7
Pub hours
Closed: No
Credit Cards: No
Chiswell St.   **Tel: 606 9158**

TRATTORIA VENEZIA
Italian ££ ●   8
12.00-15.00, 18.00-23.30
Closed Sat L. Sun
(booking advisable)
Credit Cards: A, AX, B, DC.
5 Goswell Rd.   **Tel: 253 5063**

159

Where To Eat — Islington - (Sadler's Wells)

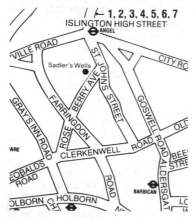

PORTOFINO
Italian-French ££ •   5
12.00-15.00, 18.00-23.30
Closed Sun (must book)
Credit Cards: A, AX, B, DC.
39 Camden Passage   **Tel: 226 1479**

TRATTORIA AQUILINO
Italian ££ •   6
Closed Sun (must book)
Credit Cards: No
31 Camden Passage   **Tel: 226 5454**

VILLA DEI PESCATORI
Fish Specialities £££ •   7
12.00-15.00, 18.00-23.30
Closed Sun (must book)
Credit Cards: A, AX, B, DC.
45 Camden Passage   **Tel: 226 7916**

CAMDEN HEAD (Pub)
Buffet £ •   1
Pub Hours
Closed No
Credit Cards: No
Camden Passage

FREDERICK'S
French £££ •   3
12.30-14.30, 19.30-23.30
Closed Sun (must book)
Credit Cards: A, AX, B, DC.
Camden Passage   **Tel: 359 2888**

MR. BUMBLE
English ££ •   4
12.30-14.30, 19.30-23.00
Closed Sun Ev. (must book)
Credit Cards: AX, B, DC.
23 Islington Green   **Tel: 354 1952**

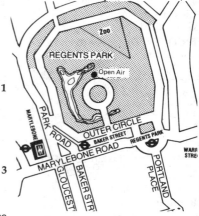

OPEN AIR THEATRE
Cold Buffet & Barbecue
18.30-22.30 £
Closed Sun
Credit Cards: No:
Bar
Pub hours

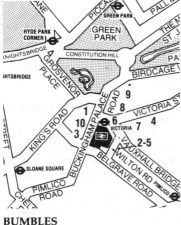

MIMMO & PASQUALE
Italian £££ ● 5
12.00-14.30, 18.30-23.00
Closed Sun (must book)
Credit Cards: All
64 Wilton Rd **Tel: 828 6908**

OVERTONS
Seafood £££ ● 6
12.00-14.30, 17.30-22.30
Closed Sun (must book)
Credit Cards: A, AX, B, DC.
4 Victoria Bldgs. **Tel: 834 3774**

PIZZA EXPRESS
Pizza £ ● 7
12.00-24.00
Closed No
Credit Cards: A, AX, B
74 Victoria St. **828 1757**

STRIKES
English ££ ● 8
11.30-23.30
Closed No
Credit Cards: A.
124 Victoria St. **Tel: 834 7350**

TAVOLA CALDA
Italian £ ● 9
12.00-23.00
Closed Sun
Credit Cards: No
3 Bressenden Place **Tel: 834 5650**

TILES (Wine Bar)
Buffet £ ● 10
12.00-15.00, 17.30-23.00
Closed Sat, Sun
Credit Cards: A, AX, B, DC.
36 Buckingham Palace Rd.
Tel: 834 7761

BUMBLES
English ££ ● 1
12.15-14.15, 18.00-22.30
Closed Sat L. Sun (must book)
Credit Cards: A, AX, B, DC.
16 Buckingham Pal. Rd. **Tel: 828 2093**

GRAN PARADISO
Italian £££ ● 2
12.00-14.30, 18.15-23.15
Closed Sat L. Sun
Credit Cards: A, AX, B, DC.
52 Wilton Road **Tel: 828 5818**

MASSIMO
Seafood-Game £££ ● 3
12.00-14.30, 18.15-23.00
Closed Sun (must book)
Credit Cards: A, AX, B, DC.
42 Buckingham Palace Rd.
Tel: 834 8283

McDONALD'S
American £ ● 4
10.00-23.00
Closed No
Credit Cards: No
155 Victoria St.

The Theatrical Capital of the World

Today, over four centuries after the opening of London's first theatre, the West End alone has some 50 theatres and concert halls (not counting fringe theatres, of which there are more than 20) ranging from the minute to the majestic, from the classical to the modern.

In the beginning

Although the Romans had introduced their own style of theatre to Britain (the remains of a Roman theatre can still be seen at St. Albans in Hertfordshire), the actual origins of our theatrical tradition can probably be attributed largely to the church. In the 10th century, priests used dramatised performances to teach bible stories and from these developed full-length 'Miracle Plays' which were presented annually to coincide with town festivals.

The early 16th century saw the emergence of the first professional actors who travelled in small groups from town to town — acting in the town squares, in the great houses of the rich and in the yards of the local inns. In 1576 London's first permanent theatre building "The Theatre" was opened in Holywell Lane, Shoreditch — pre-dating Elizabethan drama as we know it today and offering such entertainment as tumbling, vaulting, fencing and rope-dancing. Due to constant criticism from the local authorities, however, it was forced to close — and was eventually dismantled and moved, piece by piece, to Bankside, an area on the south bank of the Thames close to London Bridge.

The Globe Theatre

The materials rescued from "The Theatre" were used to build the famous Globe Theatre, the opening of which in 1599 heralded a flourishing period for live entertainment of all kinds in this part of London. Although little remains today, the fascinating Bear Gardens Museum records in great detail the character and style of the Bankside theatres.

These theatres, of course, also provided a natural outlet for such great writers of the day as Shakespeare, Marlowe and Ben Johnson. Theatre-building too, took on a new importance and was greatly influenced by continental designs. The practice of Italian courtiers of presenting their own grand form of entertainment was introduced to England by the architect Inigo Jones, whose designs for plays proved

162

extremely popular in the courts of James I and Charles I — and whose influence was to last for the next 300 years. In 1642, however, the Puritan regime introduced the Suppression of Theatres Act. Unfortunately, no theatres survived this period which lasted only until 1660 when Charles II came to the throne and encouraged a revival.

The Restoration
The first Restoration theatres were built in the Covent Garden area, which rapidly became the centre of London's theatre-land — and has remained so ever since. The most notable were built on the sites now occupied by The Theatre Royal, Drury Lane and The Royal Opera House, Covent Garden. Each has become a national institution in its own right — the former being recognised as the primary house for stage musicals and the latter for its fine operatic productions and, of course, as the home of the Royal Ballet Company.

As a result of the influx of actors, artistes and their less attractive following in the 18th and 19th centuries, the elite moved away from Covent Garden towards Mayfair — soon to be followed by an ever increasing number of West End theatres, many of which have now disappeared.

As theatres became more and more accessible to the general public and less the private preserve of the well-to-do, so the buildings increased in size, to accommodate larger audiences and to provide additional revenue for financing the more extravagant productions which were now demanded.

The Music Hall
The 19th century was also the heyday of the actor-manager — bringing fame and fortune to such as Sir Henry Irving, William Macready and Frank Benson, whose main following was among the middle classes. It was primarily to cater for the tastes of the working classes that public houses were obliged to put on entertainment — and this, in turn, led to the birth of the Music Hall. The only surviving relic is now Wilton's Music Hall, near Tower Bridge, which, it is hoped, will one day be able to re-open.

The West End Theatre today
Most of the theatres which have survived to the present day were built at the turn of the century.

Notable features of London's recent theatrical history have been The New London, the rebuilding of The Mermaid, The National Theatre on the south bank and, in 1982, the exciting new arts complex at the Barbican — which is the home of the Royal Shakespeare Company in London and the London Sympthony Orchestra.

Useful Information

Parts of the Theatre

Amphitheatre
The highest seats above the Balcony, now largely obselete.

Dress Circle
The first (lowest) circle, sometimes known as "Royal Circle". Traditionally these were the most expensive seats for which patrons wore evening dress. This is no longer the case any form of dress is acceptable throughout the theatre.

Fly Tower
The area directly above the stage from which the scenery is "flown" (or suspended) until it is needed on stage when it is lowered. In most modern theatres such machinery is worked by electricity.

Gods, The
Traditionally the gallery above or behind the Upper Circle where there were the cheapest unreserved seats. In many theatres the gallery has now been combined with the Upper Circle or balcony and unreserved seats are almost a thing of the past.

Pit
Originally the ground floor of the theatre and the cheapest part after the gallery inhabited by the 'Pittites'.

Rake
The angle of incline of the stage or seats from back to front.

Royal Box
Traditionally this is on the right hand side of the Dress Circle and is permanently reserved for Royalty wishing to attend a performance.

Stage
Since the end of the nineteenth century there have been experiments in all kinds of theatre, often reverting to the original *Open Stage* and *Theatre-in-the-Round* style of the early classical theatres. Today, theatre designs utilise modern techniques which allow theatres to be altered in shape and concept to suit the production.

Stalls
Known as "Orchestra Stalls" in America and in some West End Theatres.

Organisations

Arts Council of Great Britain, The
Founded at the beginning of the last war to organise arts activities in evacuation areas. Since 1942 has been financed by The Treasury and now gives grants to many provincial and some London theatres, as well as being involved with various theatrical training schemes and assisting with new and progressive theatrical ventures of all kinds.

British Theatre Association
Extensive reference library (& lending library for members). Tel: 01-387 2666

Equity
British Actors' Equity Association — the British actors' union which was established in 1929.

Group Sales Box Office
Party bookings for London and Broadway. Tel: 01-930 6123

Society of West End Theatre, The
The Trade Association representing, the West End Theatre owners, managers and producers. The Society actively promotes the West End Theatre by means of its publications, the Leicester Square Ticket Booth and West End Theatre gift tokens and presents its own awards — The Laurence Olivier Awards — annually to the Theatre Profession. (See pages 19, 64).

Types of Production

Command Performance
A theatrical show performed at the request of the Monarch and in his or her presence.

Farce
During the 50's and 60's Brian Rix revitalised the farce with his popular series of 'Whitehall Farces' at the Whitehall Theatre.

Melodrama
Exaggerated drama relying on lighting, music and all kinds of special effects to heighten emotion. Popular in early Victorian times but gradually declining until, by the end of the nineteenth century it actually became a derogatory term.

Pantomime
Traditional Christmas entertainment, with a fairy tale theme (which is loosely adhered to!) interspersed with popular songs, topical comedy and audience participation. In England the Principal Boy's role is usually played by a girl in tights and the comedy 'Dame' by a man.

Where to Stay

Hotels Central London

The following list includes only those hotels which are located in or around London's West End theatreland — but nevertheless offers a wide choice of recommended traditional and contemporary accommodation at all price levels. For details of hotels outside the area which offer a range of accommodation and prices comparable to those found in any major city, contact The London Tourist Board at Victoria Railway Station — where you will also be able to make your reservation. The opening hours are 9.00-22.30hrs.

Hotel ratings: ★★★★★ Luxury   ★★★★ First Class
★★★ Very Comfortable   ★★ Good Average

ATHENAEUM ★★★★   Map 3
116 Piccadilly, W1V OBJ.
Tel: 499 3464   Telex: 261589   Cable: Acropolis London W1.
Rank Hotel. 112 rooms. One of London's newer hotels, which in its design gives full consideration to a gracious and comfortable English style. The theme is continued into the restaurant with its traditional English dishes and international cuisine. The bar is reminiscent of a 19th century Club. 3 suites are designed to cater for private meetings, luncheons and dinner parties.

BERKELEY ★★★★★   Map 3
Wilton Place, SW1X 7RL
Tel: 235 6000   Telex: 919252   Cable: Silentium London SW1.
Savoy Group of Hotels. 160 rooms. Behind the modern exterior of this luxury hotel, elegance and comfort abound. Bedrooms are tastefully furnished. Amenities include swimming pool and poolside bar, saunas, massage rooms, private cinema, main Restaurant and The Buttery. Service impeccable and unobtrusive.

BERNERS ★★★   Map 1
Berners Street, W1A 3BE
Tel: 636 1629   Telex: 25759   Cable: Berners Hotel Ldn W1.
237 rooms. Built in 1909 it still retains its Edwardian elegance and charm. Lounge bar, restaurant, conference and reception facilities for 10-150.

BRITANNIA ★★★★   Map 1
Grosvenor Square W1A 3AN
Tel: 629 9400   Telex: 23941   Telefax: 629 7736
Inter-Continental. 356 rooms. Georgian style building with all modern comforts. Amenities: Anglo-American restaurant and bar, Waterloo Despatch Pub, Shogun-Japanese restaurant, piano bar, business centre, shopping arcade, conference and banqueting facilities for 120 people.

BROWN'S ★★★★ Map 3
Albemarle Street/Dover Street, W1A 4SW
Tel: 493 6020 Telex: 28686 Cable: Brownotel London W1
Trust Houses Forte. 132 rooms. One of London's traditional hotels that has maintained high standards of service and comfort. Each bedroom has its own charm and style. Of interest there is the St. George's Bar and L'Aperitif Restaurant. Private reception rooms are available for private luncheons and dinners, wedding receptions up to 150 persons.

CAVENDISH ★★★★ Map 3
Jermyn Street, SW1Y 6JF
Tel: 930 2111 Telex: 263187 Cable: Rosatel.
Trust Houses Forte. 255 rooms. In the past, the original hotel was very popular with Royalty — today ideals are kept alive in service, cuisine and atmosphere. Rebuilt in 1966, it is run with efficiency, elegance and style offering round-the-clock service. There is the Sub Rosa bar and not to be forgotten, the Cavendish Restaurant open 24 hours, 7 days a week. Private rooms cater for meetings, lunches, celebration parties and intimate dinners in an elegant style.

CHARING CROSS ★★★ Map 4
Strand, WC2N 5HX
Tel: 839 7282 Telex: 261101.
British Transport Hotels. 210 rooms. Comfortable and convenient. All bedrooms have private bath or shower. Elegant Edwardian decor in the Aperitif Bar. Comfortable elegant surrounds in the Betjeman Carving Restaurant, Jubilee and Pullman Bars. Amenities include the Sauna Club with massage and sun-ray treatment room. Banqueting and conference facilities for 150.

CHESTERFIELD ★★★★ Map 3
34-36 Charles Street, W1X 8LX
Tel: 491 2622 Telex: 269394 Cable: Chesotel London W1.
87 rooms. A 1747 gracious town house which has been redesigned into a comfortable hotel without losing the charm of the Regency period. The Terrace Bar has historical interests. Butlers Restaurant offers buffet luncheons and traditional French and English dishes for dinners.

CHURCHILL ★★★★★ Map 1
Portman Square, W1A 4ZX
Tel: 486 5800 Telex: 264831 Cable: Churchotel London W1.
489 rooms. Contemporary luxury hotel. Though large, the service is geared to individual requirements including 24-hour full menu room service. For informal meals The Greenery — and for formal occasions The Regency style Number 10. The Churchill Bar has Oriental sporting scenes around the walls and a pianist six nights a week. Elegant and varied conference and banqueting facilites for 30-350.

Hotels

CLARIDGES ★★★★★ Map 1
Brook Street, W1A 2JQ
Tel: 629 8860 Telex: 21872 Cable: Claridges
Savoy Hotels. 205 rooms. The ultimate in luxury, this hotel epitomises English tradition, with all its elegance and comfort. Frequented by Royalty, Rulers and the famous.

CLIFTON-FORD ★★★ Map 1
Welbeck Street, London W1M 8DN
Tel: 486 6600 Telex: 22569 Cable: Cliflinton London W1
Doyle London Hotels, 219 rooms. Comfortable modern hotel. Bar, Beefeater Restaurant for English Food, 24 hour room service, conference facilities.

CONNAUGHT ★★★★★ Map 1
Carlos Place, W1Y 6AL
Tel: 499 7070 Cable: Chataigne, London
90 rooms. Enjoys an International reputation for its unostentatious luxury, peaceful old Manor House charm and efficient service. The bar, restaurant and grill are renowned. Reservations way in advance advisable.

CUMBERLAND ★★★★ Map 1
Marble Arch, W1A 4RF
Tel: 262 1234 Telex: 22215 Cable: Cumberotel, London W1.
Trust Houses Forte. 910 rooms. Large modern hotel with extensive facilities. These include The Carvery for meat specialities, "The Coffee Shop" for informality, The Wyvern Restaurant for something special — and the Nocturne Bar — one of three cocktail bars. Various conference and banqueting facilities accommodating 20-330.

DORCHESTER ★★★★★ Map 3
Park Lane, W1A 2HJ
Tel: 629 8888 Telex: 887704 Cable: Dorch-Hotel London.
283 rooms. One of the worlds great luxury hotels. Whilst continuing the best traditions of British hospitality comfort and service new management is continually updating amenities and decorations. Current plans include the air-conditioning of all guest rooms. The bar provides an elegant backdrop for cocktails, light lunches and suppers while the Grill Room serves the 'Best of British' to a discriminating clientele. The hotels Terrace restaurant reflects the fine cuisine of Maitre Chef Anton Mosimann whilst many private function rooms cater for parties of 6-600. The fine reputation of this hotel has, to a great extent been built on the dedication of its staff.

DRURY LANE ★★★★ Map 2
10 Drury Lane, High Holborn, WC2B 5RE
Tel: 836 6666 Telex: 8811395 Cable: Drutel London WC2.
Grand Metropolitan. 128 rooms. One of London's newest, modern and comfortable hotels with relaxing atmosphere extended throughout. Maudie's Restaurant and Bar and 24-hour room and lounge service. Conference and banqueting facilities for 50-150.

DUKES ★★★★
Map 3
St. James' Place, SW1A 1NY
Tel: 491 4840 Telex: 28283 Cable: Dukeshotel.
56 rooms. Built in 1908, in an area of London steeped in history, pageantry and culture. Elegance is its keynote and the best of modern facilities are blended with traditional service, courtesy and decor. The Duke's Bar and St. James' Room Restaurant are widely renowned for their friendly atmosphere and fine food. An elegant banqueting suite is available for private functions.

LONDON MARRIOTT HOTEL ★★★★★
Map 1
Grosvenor Square, W1A 4AW
Tel: 493 1232 Telex: 268101 Lonmar G
Marriott Hotels and Resorts. 229 rooms. Completely refurbished during 1984 bringing this ideally situated hotel up to five star standards. Diplomat-Restaurant and Bar on Grosvenor Square and the Regent Lounge. Conference and banquet facilities for 30-500.

GROSVENOR HOUSE ★★★★★
Map 1
Park Lane, W1A 3AA
Tel: 499 6363 Telex: 24871 Cable: Grovhows London W1.
Trust Houses Forte. 478 rooms. Another traditionally famous hotel which has recently been refurbished at a cost of millions of pounds, resulting in a style of informal elegance throughout its amenities — which include the Park Lounge, Red Devil Bar, La Fontaine Restaurant and La Piazza Coffee Shop, not forgetting the exceptional indoor swimming pool, gymnasium and health club. Banqueting and conference facilities cater for up to 2,200.

HILTON ★★★★★
Map 3
Park Lane, W1A 2HH
Tel: 493 8000 Telex: 24873 Cable: Hiltels London
510 rooms. A contemporary hotel geared to today's needs whilst to a great extent retaining style and atmosphere. Used extensively for International business, a convention and meeting centre. Rooms generally large and well appointed. There are five bars and four restaurants. Well known are the Roof Restaurant for dining and supper dancing, Trader Vic's Polynesian Restaurant and the Scandinavian Sandwich Shop. Banquet and convention facilities for 50-1,000.

HOLIDAY INN MAYFAIR ★★★★★
Map 3
Berkeley St./Piccadilly/London W1X 6NE
Tel: 493 8282 Telex: 24561 Holidex: Lonmf
Holiday Inn Hotels Inc. 190 room with 7 luxurious suites. Recently refurbished throughout. Berkeley Room Restaurant, A la Carte menu, 2 Table D'Hote menus, and executive luncheon and a traditional Sunday Brunch.

HOWARD ★★★★★
Map 2
Temple Place, Strand, WC2R 2PR Tel: 836 3555 Telex: 268047
Barclays Hotel. 141 rooms. This luxury hotel, with panoramic views of the Thames has a blend of elegant decoration in its public rooms, whilst bedrooms are of modern luxury and traditional design. Cocktail bar and restaurant serving French haute cuisine. 24-hour room service.

Hotels

INN ON THE PARK ★★★★★   Map 3
Park Lane, W1A 1AZ
Tel: 499 0888 Telex: 22771 Cable: Innpark
Four Seasons Hotel. 228 rooms. This luxury hotel in a beautiful setting is one of
London's nicest hotels. The richness and comfort extend into its Guest
Lounge, Garden Room with garden patio, the famous Four Seasons
Restaurant, and the informal Lanes Restaurant. Banqueting, meetings and
reception facilities in five rooms can accommodate 40-600.

INTER-CONTINENTAL ★★★★★   Map 3
1 Hamilton Place, Hyde Park Corner, W1V OQY
Tel: 409 3131 Telex: 25853 Cable: Hydparcor
500 rooms. This luxury air conditioned hotel has the best to offer. Rooms
designed for modern confort. Seventh Floor Hamiltons Supper Club with
wonderful views over London, live entertainment and night-time disco
dancing. The Coffee House Restaurant with its 18th. century atmosphere, the
Le Soufflé Restaurant, famous for its French cuisine. Meeting rooms for
everything from a small strategy session to a conference for 750 with
simultaneous translation in the ballroom. Garage under hotel.

LONDONER ★★★   Map 1
Welbeck Street, W1M 8HS
Tel: 935 4442 Telex: 89463 Cable: Superotel London W1.
142 rooms all with private facilities. Colour television and direct dial telephones.
Amenities include a bar and Oliver's Restaurant. Also 24 hour lounge and
Room Service.

LONDONDERRY ★★★★★   Map 3
Park Lane, W1Y 8AP
Tel: 493 7292 Telex: 263292.
140 rooms. A modern well appointed hotel with comfortable and attractive
rooms. The Isle de France Restaurant has a beautiful circular setting under a
draped tented ceiling. 24-hour Coffee Shop.

MANDEVILLE ★★★★   Map 1
Mandeville Place, London W1M 6BE
Tel: 935 5599 Telex: 2469487 Cables: Manvilhote London W1.
Executive Hotels. 163 bedrooms all with bath and shower, well furnished,
colour television with free in-house movies, dial direct telephone etc.,
Boswell's pub, La Cocotte Cocktail Bar, Orangery Coffee House, La Cocotte
Mediterranean a la carte restaurant, 24-hour lounge and room service.

MAYFAIR ★★★★★   Map 3
Berkeley Street, W1A 2AN
Tel: 629 7777 Telex: 262526 Cable: Mayfairtel London W1.
Grand Metropolitan. 330 rooms. One of London's older hotels, well known for
its amenities and comfort. The Chateaubriand Restaurant for good food and
elegant dinning, 9 banqueting suites, the Mayfair Theatre which seats 310 for
special events and the Starlight Cinema.

MOSTYN ★★★　　　　　　　　　　　　　　　　　　　Map 1
Portman Street, W1H 0DE
Tel: 935 2361 Telex: 27656 Cable: Mostyno London W1.
Grand Metropolitan. 107 rooms, tastefully furnished, most with separate bathroom and shower. Brummells Bar and Restaurant. Banqueting and conference facilities for 10-100.

MOUNT ROYAL ★★★　　　　　　　　　　　　　　　Map 1
Marble Arch, W1A 4UR
Tel: 629 8040 Telex: 23355 Cable: Mounroy London W1.
Mount Charlotte Hotels. 700 rooms. Well decorated spacious rooms, all with private bathroom and shower and colour TV. Harry's Bar, Coffee House and Terrace Grill Restaurant. Conference and banqueting facilities for 1,500.

PARK LANE ★★★★　　　　　　　　　　　　　　　　Map 3
Tel: 499 6321 Telex: 21533 Cable: Parlanotel Piccadilly, W1Y 8BX
54 suites and 270 rooms. One of London's older and more traditional hotels. All bedrooms have a bathroom en suite, double glazing, direct dial telephone, mini bar, colour television, radio and 24 hour room service. Bracewells and the Garden Room Restaurants, The Bar and The Palm Court Lounge. Banqueting and conference facilities for up to 600. Private garage for 180 cars.

PASTORIA ★★★　　　　　　　　　　　　　　　　　Map 2
St Martin's Street, WC2H 7HL
Tel: 930 8641 Telex: 25538 Cable: Heartowest London WC2.
Independant. 52 rooms. A small friendly hotel with a family atmosphere and comfortable bedrooms. Bar and lounge are pleasant for relaxing, with tasty snacks served in the restaurant.

PICCADILLY ★★★★　　　　　　　　　　　　　　　Map 2
Tel: 734 8000 Telex: 25795 Cable: Piqudilo London W1. Piccadilly, W1V 0BH
Forum Hotels. 290 rooms. Built in 1909, much of the grandeur of the past has been retained in this traditional hotel. The spacious bedrooms are all with private bath and tastefully furnished. Edwardian style Carver's Table Restaurant is known for its hot and cold roast meats and the Press Bar as a good meeting place. There are dining facilities for 450 and conference facilities for 600.

PORTMAN (Situated in the heart of theatre land) **★★★★**　　Map 1
22 Portman Square, W1H 9FL
Tel: 486 5844 Telex: 261526 Cable: Inhotelcor.
Inter-Continental. 278 rooms. Fully air-conditioned rooms with mini-bars, colour television, free in-house movies, and built in hairdryers in all bathrooms. 24-hour room service. Portman Corner — Pub and Bakery, Truffles French Restaurant. Bar Normande, Rotisserie Normand. Conference facilities for up to 600 persons.

REGENT PALACE ★★　　　　　　　　　　　　　　Map 1
Piccadilly Circus, W1R 6EP
Tel: 734 7000 Telex: 23740 Cable: Regentotle
Trust Houses Forte. 1,002 rooms. Busy, very popular and well run with friendly atmosphere. Many bars and restaurants including the Carvery.

Hotels

TIIE RITZ (Deluxe) ★★★★★ Map 3
Piccadilly, W1V 9DG
Tel: 493 8181 Telex: 267200 Cable: Ritzotel.
141 rooms. Being restored to its former magnificence with modern amenities, skilfully blended with the traditional splendour. The renowned high standard of service is being maintained. Experience the sheer beauty of the Palm Court for afternoon tea. The Restaurant, with its beautiful decor and lavish ceiling paintings has always been the rendezvous of important figures from all walks of life.

ROYAL ADELPHI ★★ Map 4
21-23 Villiers Street, WC2N 6ND.
Tel: 930 8764
55 rooms. Situated next to Charing Cross Station — inexpensive catering for the tourist, and businessman.

ROYAL ANGUS ★★★ Map 2
39 Coventry Street, Piccadilly Circus, W1V 8EL
Tel: 930 4033 Telex: 24616
Thistle Hotel. 92 rooms. Comfortable rooms. Modern design. Cocktail Bar and Coffee Shop.

ROYAL HORSEGUARDS ★★★★ Map 4
2A Whitehall Court, SW1A 2EJ
Tel: 839 3400 Telex: 917096
Thistle Hotel. 280 rooms. Smart, well furnished with modern comforts. Spacious lounge, Granby's Restaurant and river front terrace. Conference and reception facilities.

ROYAL TRAFALGAR THISTLE HOTEL ★★★ Map 4
Whitcomb St, Trafalgar Square, WC2H 7HG
Tel: 01-930 4477 Telex: 24616
108 rooms, modern hotel used by businessmen and tourists. Has its own English Pub, Lounge and new Brasserie and Cocktail Bar.

SAVOY ★★★★★ Map 2
Strand, WC2R OEU
Tel: 836 4343 Telex: 24234
200 rooms. Luxurious and renowned for its excellence throughout. 24-hour room service is only one of its many special services. Conference and entertaining facilities range from most intimate and elegant private dining rooms to the Lancaster Room which accommodates 500 people. The Savoy Theatre is part of this complex.

ST. GEORGE'S ★★★★ Map 1
Langham Place, Oxford Circus, W1N 8QS
Tel: 580 0111 Telex: 27274 Cable: St. George's Hotel London W1.
Trust House Forte (U.K.) Ltd. 85 rooms. Modern most comfortable tower-like construction with excellent view of the City from public rooms. The Summit Restaurant on the 14th floor is renowned for its good food.

Hotels

STAFFORD ★★★★
Map 3
16 St. James's Place, SW1A 1NJ
Tel: 493 0111 Telex: 28602 Cable: Staforotel.
61 rooms. Peacefully situated, this converted mansion offers the best in English tradition. Gracefully furnished throughout. American Bar and Restaurant of high repute. Banqueting facilities for 10-50.

STRAND PALACE ★★★
Map 2
Strand, WC2R OJJ
Tel: 836 8080 Telex: 24208 Cable: Luxury London WC2R OJJ
Trust House Forte. 770 rooms. Large practical and convenient hotel with all the necessary amenities, well known cocktail bar, coffee shop, Carvery for fixed price meals, hot and cold buffet, Italian Connection restaurant off Covent Garden with Pizzeria, Piazza and R'Osteria Bar. Conference and entertainment facilities for 20-200.

STRATFORD COURT ★★
Oxford Street, W1N 0BY
Tel: 629 7474 Telex: 22270 Cable: Strafort London W1.
134 rooms. Modern and comfortable bedrooms, each with private bathroom and shower. Cocktail bar and Bib and Tucker Restaurant.

WALDORF ★★★★
Map 2
Aldwych, WC2B 4DD
Tel: 936 2400 Telex: 24574 Cable: Waldorfius
Trust House Forte. 310 rooms. An Edwardian style hotel which has recently been carefully redecorated to retain its original elegance. Well appointed public rooms, bars, well known Palm Court Lounge and Wellington Restaurant. Conference and reception facilities are varied and numerous, 12-400.

WASHINGTON ★★★
5/7 Curzon Street, W1Y 8DT
Tel: 499 7030 Telex: 24540 Cable: Georgotel London W1
Sarova Hotels. 159 rooms. Public rooms are pleasant and comfortable. La Fayette Restaurant and 4th Hussars Bar. Conference and reception facilities for 30-250.

WESTBURY ★★★★
Map 1
New Bond Street at Conduit Street, London W1A 4UH
Tel: 01-629 7755 Telex: 24378
A luxury hotel situated in the heart of fashionable Mayfair. 242 bedrooms including 14 suites. All rooms have private bath and shower, remote control colour television, direct dial telephone, 24 hour room service. Public rooms include Polo bar, Restaurant and 24 hour lounge. Conference and banqueting suites available to accommodate from 10-100 people.

INDEX—Where To Eat

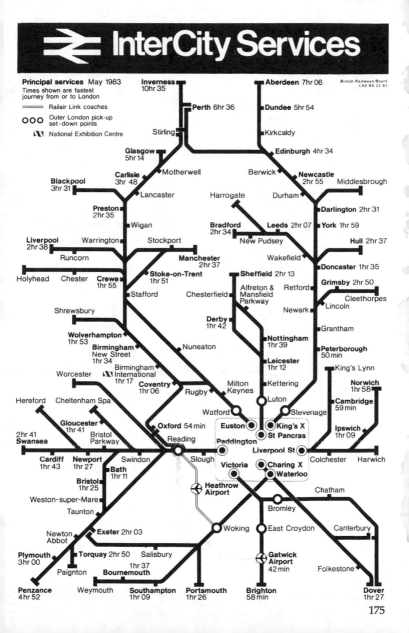

InterCity Services

Principal services May 1983
Times shown are fastest
journey from or to London

═══ Railair Link coaches

OOO Outer London pick-up
set-down points

◥◣ National Exhibition Centre

British Railways Board
CAS 'BS 22 83

Inverness 10hr 35
Perth 6hr 36
Stirling
Glasgow 5hr 14
Motherwell
Carlisle 3hr 48
Lancaster
Blackpool 3hr 31
Preston 2hr 35
Wigan
Liverpool 2hr 38
Warrington
Runcorn
Holyhead Chester Crewe 1hr 55
Stockport
Manchester 2hr 37
Stoke-on-Trent 1hr 51
Stafford
Shrewsbury
Wolverhampton 1hr 53
Birmingham New Street 1hr 34
Worcester
Birmingham International 1hr 17
Nuneaton
Coventry 1hr 06
Hereford Cheltenham Spa
Gloucester 1hr 41
Bristol Parkway
2hr 41 Swansea
Cardiff 1hr 43
Newport 1hr 27
Swindon
Bath 1hr 11
Bristol 1hr 25
Weston-super-Mare
Taunton
Newton Abbot
Exeter 2hr 03
Plymouth 3hr 00
Torquay 2hr 50
Paignton
Penzance 4hr 52
Weymouth
Salisbury
Bournemouth 1hr 37
Southampton 1hr 09
Portsmouth 1hr 26

Aberdeen 7hr 06
Dundee 5hr 54
Kirkcaldy
Edinburgh 4hr 34
Berwick
Newcastle 2hr 55
Middlesbrough
Harrogate
Durham
Darlington 2hr 31
Bradford 2hr 34
Leeds 2hr 07
York 1hr 59
New Pudsey
Hull 2hr 37
Wakefield
Doncaster 1hr 35
Sheffield 2hr 13
Grimsby 2hr 50
Alfreton & Mansfield Parkway
Chesterfield
Retford
Cleethorpes
Newark
Lincoln
Derby 1hr 42
Grantham
Nottingham 1hr 39
Peterborough 50 min
Leicester 1hr 12
King's Lynn
Kettering
Milton Keynes
Luton
Stevenage
Norwich 1hr 58
Cambridge 59 min
Ipswich 1hr 09
Watford
Euston King's X
St Pancras
Paddington
Liverpool St
Colchester Harwich
Victoria Charing X
Waterloo
Reading
Slough
Heathrow Airport
Chatham
Bromley
Woking East Croydon
Canterbury
Gatwick Airport 42 min
Folkestone
Brighton 58 min
Dover 1hr 27

Oxford 54 min
Rugby

Transport

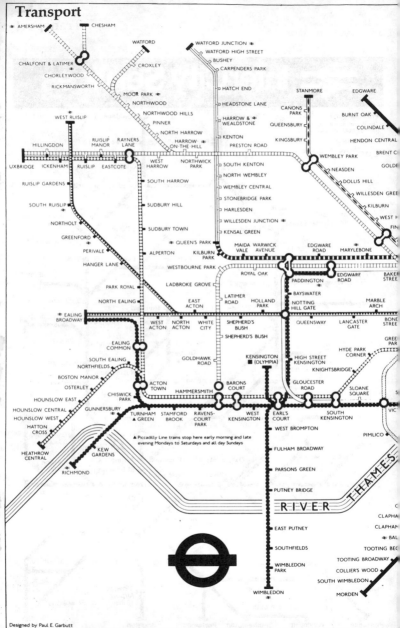

Designed by Paul E. Garbutt
Copyright London Transport Executive